NOTORIOUS HUNTER
SIR ST. GEORGE GORE

Deadly Legacy in Colorado

JOHN LACONTE
With Photography by Scott Cramer

THE History PRESS

Published by The History Press
An imprint of Arcadia Publishing
Charleston, SC
www.historypress.com

Front cover: Sir St. George Gore with punt gun. *Andrew Oldin.*

First published 2025

Manufactured in the United States

ISBN 9781467159982
Hardcover ISBN 9781540299857

Library of Congress Control Number: 2025941216

To my mother, Sandy LaConte,
who never lets a question go without a thorough investigation.

CONTENTS

ACKNOWLEDGMENTS

My foremost appreciation goes out to all the writers and editors who kept Sir St. George Gore's legend alive over the years. A great many raconteurs realized how good Gore's story was and felt that the memories of his expedition were worth the work it took to put them into print. Now, 150 years later, digitization has shown that print didn't die as predicted—it grew stronger, making the records of our past more accessible than ever.

But that, too, took an immense amount of work, so I must acknowledge my deep indebtedness to the teams of developers, archivists and, most importantly, public fundraising entities like History Colorado and local groups like the Vail Public Library, the Eagle Valley Library District and the many others that have helped see to the digitization of the old newspapers published in their towns. In Colorado, the state's historic newspaper archive is a public resource, free to use, and the access it provides has completely changed the way I now approach my job as a reporter.

My editor Nate Peterson was the first person who suggested that the Sir St. George Gore story I had stumbled upon might be worthy of a longer work. Many editors would have, upon learning of never-reported details involving a namesake in their town, insisted those stories come out in their newspaper first, but Nate told me it sounded like something that would make a good book. He also told me to ask Kathy Heicher with the Eagle Valley Historical Society for help, and she suggested some sources and referred me to The History Press, which promptly accepted my proposal. To that end,

I'm thankful to have been assigned to editor Laurie Krill at The History Press, as she embraced the idea and was encouraging throughout the process.

My wife, Polina, and my kids, Lilia and John John, after spending a night with me in a tent on Gore Pass during the summer of 2023, started asking a lot of great questions about Gore when we visited his plaque and found it to be vandalized. When I suggested to Polina that I might pitch a Gore biography to a few publishers, she agreed that it would be something she would like to see in print as a reader of adventure stories herself, and she encouraged me to write the book despite the extra domestic work she foresaw this distraction creating in our home. Much of that work landed in her lap, which she took on without complaint, but my parents also came into town to help with the kids as my deadline approached, which was very helpful. My parents have always been incredibly supportive of my writing, even after they caught me living in my car in California while working a low-paying journalism job. They never told me to stop and instead repeated the mantra that captures the essence of reporting: if you think there's something there, just keep going.

My good friend Jake Blair, through his many hours of listening to me discuss Gore, helped me see the larger themes present in the story, and my lifelong pal Dan Peterson reminded me of the expression that's used in the epilogue of this story, which perfectly embodies Gore and his legacy. Researcher Jennifer Mitten helped me find information on the ships that carried Gore to and from North America. Jerry Enzler, the author of Jim Bridger's most recent biography, shared some of his research and contacts with me and was also very encouraging. Jamie Gaukroger with High Life Highland was helpful in finding photos of Gore's old haunts in Scotland. Scott Cramer's photographic mastery captures the immense beauty of the many landmarks that bear Gore's name; I'm so thankful that he offered to collaborate. Local illustrator Andrew Oldin took on the cover art with a zeal for the assignment, his only motivation being the fact that he loved hearing old tales about Colorado and wanted to see a cover that reflected the compelling nature of Gore's story. His interest in the project motivated me to keep going, as well.

PROLOGUE

A lot of curiosity about Sir St. George Gore, the eighth baronet of Manor Gore in Northern Ireland, has emerged since he journeyed from the United Kingdom to the United States in the 1850s, embarking on a massive Rocky Mountain odyssey.

Among the questions: Who might have inspired his journey? What route did he take to reach the Rockies? When did he arrive and leave? Where are all the places he visited before and after his trip out west? How did he become the namesake of so many landmarks in Colorado?

This book will provide answers to all of those previously unanswered questions, but the big one still persists: Why? Why did Gore want to leave behind his lavish lifestyle and retreat into the mountains for three years? And that one is a little tougher to answer. The man kept no journals that we know of, he led a private lifestyle and he doesn't appear to have discussed his inspirations with anyone who might have taken them down in a book or journal. He was unmarried and had no children, and no family lore appears to have survived about him following the death of the second of his two sisters in 1904.

The previously untapped material I've discovered sheds light on how he spent his time and his money and where his passions were directed, but his motivations remain a mystery.

Some of what I've discovered about Gore has been hiding in plain sight, and I'm surprised that it hasn't yet been revealed to become part of his story. The fact that he was one of Ireland's notorious absentee landlords during the Great Famine is one of those details that's seldom discussed about Gore, but it would be somewhat obvious if something as simple as a Wikipedia page was ever created about him. Wikipedia currently lists all the winners of the Waterloo Cup coursing competitions, and Gore's name is listed there in both 1848 and 1849. So, if a page would have been created and connected to that event, it may have made obvious the fact that Gore was in England, entering coursing competitions, while his lands in Ireland were being ravaged by mass starvation.

Winning the Waterloo Cup—in back-to-back years no less—is a rare feat indeed. It's a big detail when it comes to Gore's legacy, big enough that it had me thinking about it for quite some time. There was so much information available about those competitions (in which dogs face off to see which can catch a rabbit first) that I began to develop a nagging feeling that maybe there was something more there, something that might even help me get to the bigger questions about Gore, if I just kept looking.

And sure enough, eventually something did occur to me in the most unlikely of places—the names of his dogs. Gore seemed to choose names that were a bit unusual when compared to his contemporaries. Why was he naming his dogs Cytherea and Pyrrhus while the men he was competing against used names like Fair Toes, Scarlet Runner and Deer Stalker? In looking at the names of Gore's other dogs—Hermione, Pallas, Agamemnon, Olympus—a pattern began to emerge: he was naming his dogs after figures from Greek folklore.

What conclusions can we draw from this? For one, it's safe to say Gore enjoyed classical mythology. And what were some of the themes of those myths? Heroes, marvelous achievements and, of course, adventure.

So, maybe that gets to the *why* of the whole thing. Maybe he longed to be part of an eventful journey akin to those in the adventure stories he read. Maybe Gore wanted to be the hero of his own Greek odyssey.

1

THE BLUE-BLOODED ROOSTER

The stench of boozy breath filled the foyer of the St. James Hotel in Jacksonville as a worn-out-looking wanderer waited for a room during the spring of 1874.

The wanderer kept his hands in his pockets, per the instructions of the night watchman, a worker named Kingsbury, who suspected the man to be a luggage thief based on his appearance—sunburned face, bloodshot eyes, torn coat and dirty pants. But the wanderer knew how to write, as evidenced by his signature in the register, which Kingsbury didn't bother to scan. The simple fact that the man was aware he should place his name there upon arrival showed the night watchman that this wanderer had most likely stayed in a hotel before, so there was a chance he was indeed looking for a room and might have even conjured up enough cash to pay for it.

But it was midnight, the perfect time for a luggage thief to prey upon the hotel, which was the largest in the southeastern United States. The area would occasionally receive some distinguished guests off the train from Savannah, tourists and sportsmen who would stalk the nearby swamps, sightseeing and searching for big game. A few months earlier, the town was abuzz with the news of a visit from a British nobleman who was the guest of Colonel George McGinly, the owner of the nearby Grand National Hotel. The St. James's owner, Deacon J.R. Campbell, was extremely envious of the visit, as the Grand National and the St. James had been in contention over which was classier and visits like the nobleman's had served to only raise the reputation of the rival property. The rumor in town was that the deacon hadn't smiled once the entire time the nobleman was in Jacksonville.

A mountain goat grazes in the Gore Range in Colorado. *Scott Cramer.*

The city's propensity to attract prominent guests, along with the late hour, only compounded Kingsbury's suspicions. A few minutes earlier, the deacon had personally shown the visitors from the late train to their rooms, and now, Kingsbury was left in charge and did not want an incident of theft to occur during his watch. Kingsbury found the deacon and asked him which room he should show the wanderer, whom he described to his boss as "a drunken old Irishman" based on his scent and accent. The wanderer had asked if the hotel had any "rooms," plural, but Kingsbury had dismissed the request for him to review multiple dwellings, and the deacon instructed Kingsbury to show the wanderer to room 40, the hotel's worst apartment, which was cramped and dusty, with a cracked wash pitcher.

Kingsbury ran quickly back to the lobby, nervous that the wanderer might have disappeared along with some of the bags from the luggage room, but he was still there, waiting with his hands in his pockets as instructed. The Florida air was balmy and stagnant, intensifying the smell of alcohol escaping the wanderer's pores. Outside the hotel's open windows, whippoorwills could be heard twittering about. Perhaps they were still in a stir from the late train's recent activity, or maybe there were more people outside, keeping the birds active.

The wanderer didn't like the room.

"I must tell you that this won't do," he said. "I want a larger apartment, one that is well furnished and with superior accommodations."

"Oh, you do, eh?" replied Kingsbury, glancing at the man with derision. "I suppose you would like the ladies' parlor? You can consider yourself mighty lucky to get this room. If I was the proprietor, I would hoist you into the hay-mow."

The wanderer stared at the watchman in perfect surprise. Several seconds passed before he could catch his breath.

"I'm greatly obliged to ye for your impertinence," he said. "But if I can't find accommodations here, I must go where I can find them."

"That's right, old fellow," Kingsbury responded. "You better go to the Grand National. That's the place for such slouchy old roosters as you."

The wanderer walked down the stairs, followed by the watchman. As he approached the doors, the wanderer was met by a half-dozen men who had slowly been making their way down the street due to the large amount of luggage they were hauling.

"Hold on, boys," the wanderer said. "This is too aristocratic for yous. The National is the place for such slouchy old roosters."

They left the lodge at once. Two large express wagons loaded with trunks traveled in their wake. The whippoorwills laughed at them as they passed under the water oaks that shaded the public square.

The next morning, the deacon greeted Kingsbury early.

"How's your drunken Irishman this morning?" the deacon asked. "Is he up yet?"

Kingsbury told the deacon that room 40 wasn't suitable for the old rooster, so he sent him packing to the Grand National instead. The deacon approached the register and began reading the names and hometowns of the night's arrivals. The final entry on the list jumped out at him.

"Sir George Gore, England," it said.

The deacon immediately recognized the name as that of the same nobleman who had been in town at the Grand National earlier that year. He grabbed his hat and ran to the rival hotel, where he saw the colonel supervising his men as they transferred large trunks to the property's most elegant rooms above. The deacon sent a card to Gore, apologizing for the mix-up and asking him to return to his hotel. But Gore's response was that he would not consider returning to the St. James, as the National was "good enough for a slouchy old rooster" such as himself.

The preceding narrative has been adapted, word for word in some parts, from newspapers that ran variations of a piece that originally appeared in the long-defunct newspaper *The Sun* in New York, which ran this story in May 1874. *The Sun* had a Florida correspondent who heard the tale and recounted it in long form; it was then picked up by several other outlets across the country.

"The story got out, and threw Jacksonville into convulsions," *The Sun* reported. "Of the ten thousand tourists in Florida the past winter, Sir George was the only one who attracted universal attention."[1]

When Gore placed his name in the St. James's directory, he was already a legend in the western United States. A mountain range in the Colorado Territory was being referred to as "Gore's Range," and a road through the northern tip of that range had been named Gore's Pass. This occurred after Gore, guided by well-known mountain man Jim Bridger, blazed a wagon trail through an existing footpath in 1854, removing trees and widening the singletrack enough to accommodate his massive hunting party, complete with fourteen wagons and forty men.[2]

The first time the words "Gore's Pass" pop up in Colorado Territory newspapers is 1861,[3] and the first printed reference of Gore's Range occurs in 1868.[4] In 2025, we can say this with confidence, as much of the state's nineteenth-century newspaper library has been digitized and is searchable. The same can be said for newspapers across the globe; indeed, we have now ushered in a golden age of research opportunities for writers like me who are interested in figures from the past.

Gore is a figure from the past who has never ceased to entice, as evidenced by his many nicknames—the Noblest Roamer, the Celtic Nimrod of the Old West or, the simplest albeit incorrect title by which he's most commonly known, Lord Gore. But most writers have been so focused on the Hollywood-esque story of his 1850s hunting expedition that they've missed not only his visit to the Southeast years later but also, and more importantly, his contribution to Ireland's Great Famine years before.

Most of the details of that Western safari, which resulted in the naming of Gore Pass and many other Colorado landmarks, can be traced back to just three sources, a fact that vexed Gore's previous biographer, Barry C. Johnson of the English Westerners' Society, who assigned another nickname to Gore, "Baronet in an Earth Lodge," in his book's title.

"All efforts to find new and substantial materials have failed—almost certainly none will now be found," Johnson wrote.[5]

But that was 1997, too early to imagine a world in which optical character recognition would make the books and newspapers of the past as searchable as the online articles of today. Thanks to that technology, we now have more than one hundred new sources to add to the Gore legacy. In addition to answering many of the questions Johnson posed in his book, the new sources offer several other interesting stories, like the one told previously, which gave Gore another nickname: the Blue-Blooded Rooster.

2
THE MARK FROM MONTREAL

The story of Sir St. George Gore as a suspected luggage thief is especially ironic because Gore himself had been a mark for luggage thieves while he was traveling through the United States two decades earlier.

On that Western expedition, which resulted in Gore becoming the namesake of the Gore Range and many other landmarks in Colorado, it has long been pondered how Gore arrived in North America from Great Britain and how he occupied his time in the United States prior to the first-known mention of him in St. Louis in March 1854.

Today, thanks to the wonders of digitization, we now know.

Gore left Liverpool on June 16, 1853, aboard the *Lady Eglinton* steamship, traveling with four servants in his company.[6] The *Lady Eglinton* was brand new at the time, constructed in Scotland and built for speed.[7] Gore was likely in the company of his own class on the voyage, which journeyed from Liverpool to the Port of Saint John in just eight days.[8] Gore then traveled through Quebec and into Montreal on the *Lady Eglinton* and hunted in the Great Lakes region before he headed south through Illinois into Missouri.[9]

In early December 1853, several newspapers noted Gore's arrival in St. Louis, reporting that his party had concluded a hunting expedition near Lake Michigan and were headed south with the intention of wintering in Texas. It was also reported that a portmanteau chest was stolen from Gore somewhere in Illinois while he was en route to St. Louis from Chicago.

The portmanteau contained "a draft for a thousand pounds, or $5,000, a signet ring, near $300 in gold, and some jewelry of value," *The St. Louis News* reported in December 1853. "While traveling in the train to Alton, [Gore] carried the portmanteau with him in the passenger car, and arriving at Springfield, got out; but, misunderstanding the time allowed for the stoppage of the train, he did not return to the station until the cars had gone. The package was stolen between Springfield and Alton, or at the latter place."[10]

Undeterred, Gore continued making plans for his winter hunting trip to the South, and a couple of weeks later, he received a shipment in St. Louis, *The Missouri Republican* reported, containing "twenty-three assorted dogs."

The newsmen were intrigued.

"Capt. John Russell, the clerk, informed us that they were the property of a party of English gentlemen from Canada, who were on their way to Texas, for the purpose of spending the winter there in hunting," the *Republican* reported.[11]

Gore then stayed out of the news until February of 1854, when *The St. Louis Intelligencer* updated the community on his endeavors.

"A few months since we noticed the arrival in this city of Sir George Gore, an Irish baronet of distinction and very fond of hunting and other wild sports," the *Intelligencer* reported in February 1854. "The gentleman had with him a large retinue of hunters, guns, fishing tackle, &e, and after spending a few days in the city he pursued his way South, with the intention of spending the winter in Texas or Mexico, since which time we have learned nothing of his whereabouts."

Along with the interesting suggestion that Gore might have made it as far south as Mexico before beginning his Western expedition, the *Intelligencer* discovered how Gore had received much of the extravagant equipment he carted through the American West. Gore's futuristic hunting accoutrements were what would go on to give him his legendary status, but it has never been known how he got all that gear into the United States.

In February 1854, the *Intelligencer* learned that a commission house in St. Louis had received a bill of lading for three vans, "sort of powder wagon concerns, a traveling carriage, a boat, and a 'hull' lot of camp and traveling 'fixings,' which were shipped by order of the hunting baronet, from Liverpool," the paper reported.

The paper estimated that Gore spent $400 on the shipment via the *Saranak No. 2* ship from New Orleans, along with another $425 on custom house dues and another $400 on the freight from Liverpool to New Orleans. The *Intelligencer* continued by ridiculing Gore on the setup, saying that, according to a Western hunter in contact with the paper, "the whole batch, boat and all, would not be valued at more than four hundred cents—the boat or float is built purposely for crossing rivers or other streams, and is of dimensions

A view of St. Louis in 1854, by Emile B. Krausse and George Hofmann. *Missouri Historical Society.*

DRESDEN
PACKET
GARDEN CITY

to admit of taking on board the traveling carriage, and the wagons perhaps not more than one or two at a time."

The *Intelligencer*'s final conclusions on Gore were published a couple of weeks ahead of a March 1854 bank draft he signed for $9,000 out of St. Louis. That banknote has always been, prior to my research, the first-known mention of Gore in the United States, which is unfortunate since the *Intelligencer*'s story leads so well into that banknote.

"The idea of shipping hunting wagons and carriages, and above all a boat, a regular 'broadhorn' across the Atlantic is certainly original, if not very expensive," the *Intelligencer* concluded. "Hang the expense, Sir George has perhaps 'lots more powder.'"[12]

It's a perfect segue into what was previously the first-known mention of Gore in the United States, the March 1854 bank draft, because the paper's prediction that Gore had more "powder," or money to spend, was then proven to be correct by that bank draft.

Gore is said to have been inspired to visit the West by fellow British baronet Sir William Drummond Stewart, who took numerous hunting and trapping trips out west in the 1830s and 1840s, and Lord Charles William Wentworth Fitzwilliam, who was just wrapping up a journey throughout the western United States as Gore was beginning his. It's long been assumed that Fitzwilliam accompanied Gore on part of his expedition, and while it's likely that they met up in St. Louis at some point, Fitzwilliam was reported back in England before Gore had departed the modern-day Kansas City area, so he most definitely didn't accompany Gore into the Rocky Mountains.

As Gore was getting ready to journey west out of St. Louis, Fitzwilliam was arriving in the city after completing his expedition. Fitzwilliam had been hunting in the West, making it as far as the Pacific Northwest in addition to visiting places like Fort Laramie in present-day Wyoming and Bent's New Fort in present-day Colorado. *The St. Louis Republican* reported on Fitzwilliam's arrival into St. Louis in March 1854[13] as he was on his way home to England, eventually being reported back in May 1854.[14]

It's likely Fitzwilliam and Gore met up before Fitzwilliam departed—in an 1897 letter to *The Denver Evening Post*, mountain man Henry Chatillon wrote that he recalled seeing Gore and Fitzwilliam together in St. Louis[15]—with Fitzwilliam possibly recommending places for Gore to visit. We know Gore journeyed to Fort Laramie not long after Fitzwilliam was there, and if Gore sought to visit Bent's New Fort as well, it could explain why some reports, including Chatillon's letter, have Gore visiting much more of Colorado than he is given credit for today.

3

KANSAS CITY COMPANIONS

After setting off from St. Louis for the Rocky Mountains in the spring of 1854, Sir St. George Gore spent time in the modern-day Kansas City area, where he got on well with some of the locals.

This is one of several previously unknown details about Gore's journey west that can now be discovered thanks to the digitization of old newspaper archives. In this case, we can thank *The Kansas City Star*, which ran stories featuring Gore in 1906 and 1912.

It has long been known that Gore made his way from St. Louis to Westport in modern-day Kansas City, as that's the origin of what was previously regarded as "the only known contemporary newspaper description" of Gore's expedition.[16] That 1854 article said Gore departed Westport with forty to fifty dogs and approximately a dozen large wagons,[17] and since then, that's all we've really known about Gore's time in the Kansas City area. Today, however, the *Star*'s digitization allows us to find other previously undiscovered accounts from his time in Westport. Among them is a 1912 story in which the paper profiled William Johnson, the oldest known Kansas-born settler at the time.

"One of Mr. Johnson's most interesting reminisces is of a visit to the camp of Sir George Gore, the famous Irish sportsman and big game hunter, who came from his estates in Sligo in the spring of 1854 to hunt buffalo and bear in America," the *Star* reported on December 15, 1912.

"My father and I were out riding one morning and came up on his encampment near the cottonwood springs just west of the mission," Johnson was quoted as saying.

A view of the Shawnee Methodist Mission, North Building, circa 1940. *Lester Jones, Library of Congress.*

Johnson was referring to the Shawnee Mission, where he was born in 1845.

"Sir George had an outfit as large or larger than that which Roosevelt took with him to Africa," Johnson recalled.[18]

Some of the tales of Gore's luxury outfit that have been called into question by more modern writers are supported by Johnson's recollections. For many years, the only study of Gore which was scholarly—with citations—was written by professor Clarke C. Spence in 1959, titled "A Celtic Nimrod in the Old West." Spence took issue with a description of Gore published by *The Cattleman Magazine* in 1952, which described Gore's party as including "imported serving men in costly livery and powdered wigs" and "fine sterling silver mugs."[19] Spence wrote that the luxuries described by the magazine "may not have existed, but if they did, documentation is lamentably lacking."[20]

But Spence doesn't appear to be aware of *The Kansas City Star*'s 1912 dispatch from Johnson, which supports *The Cattleman*'s reporting:

> *When we came up Lord Gore came out of his tent, greeted us and invited us to take breakfast with him. My father declined and Sir George then insisted that I should stay and take breakfast with them, and my father consented. It must be remembered that Kansas was then a part of the*

> *wilderness and it was indeed a strange sight to see Sir George maintaining the social customs of a British lord, with solid silver service and white linen on the table, and more the wonder drew when liveried servants with powdered hair and knee breeches and silver buckles on their shoes, came and stood behind our respective chairs and served breakfast. I have never seen anything as stylish since.*[21]

Johnson's father, Reverend Thomas Johnson, was the founder of the Shawnee Mission, otherwise known as the Shawnee Indian Manual Labor Boarding School, where Johnson was born. Johnson's father was a Methodist minister who was born in Virginia and moved to Missouri, where he agreed with the U.S. government's assessment that a school needed to be built for the purposes of "instructing the Indian Children the arts of mechanism as well as that of literature."[22]

The Shawnee Mission was one of "more than 400 boarding schools in 37 states designed to culturally assimilate indigenous children in the United States," writes the National Trust for Historic Preservation, "a practice of forced labor and mistreatment of children as young as four years old, that often included physical and emotional abuse. Complete erasure of their cultural identity was the goal."

In 2021, the National Trust for Historic Preservation started working with the Shawnee tribe to have the Shawnee Mission land conveyed to the tribe. The site of Johnson's Shawnee Mission, in the area where Gore visited in the spring of 1854, is currently a National Historic Landmark, and the land is owned by the City of Fairway in Kansas. Shawnee Chief Ben Barnes told the National Trust for Historic Preservation that the school is a memorial to the struggles and perseverance of the Native youth who attended the school.

"We can still see carvings on the wall, left in the windowless attics where children were forced to sleep in hot summers and cold winters," Barnes said.[23]

Gore, who would go on to have a mountain range in Colorado named after him, and Johnson, who has a county named after him in Kansas, had much in common. A few years earlier, on Gore's land in Ireland, a national school had been set up for the children of the Irish tenants who toiled on his property. Not unlike the Native boarding schools in the United States, the national schools of Ireland were set up with assimilation in mind.

The national schools of Ireland instructed children in English rather than their native Irish and taught the children to have respect for authority and loyalty to the British Crown. Not only were Irish history, cultural identity and heritage ignored, a basic understanding of Irish geography was also not even a part of the curriculum.

Just as Gore received money from the British government to create his school, Johnson also received funds from a society created following the 1819 Civilization Fund Act in the United States. The language used in the act said its aim was to "civilize" the country's Native populations, but the true intent is better described by the National Native American Boarding School Healing Coalition, which said the act worked in concert with the Christian church "to implement cultural genocide through the removal and reprogramming of American Indian and Alaska Native children to accomplish the systematic destruction of Native cultures and communities."[24]

A recently uncovered letter from Shawnee leadership, dated February 21, 1860, described Johnson's neglect in failing to ensure the school had humane living conditions for the students despite the funds allotted to him.

"This whole sum is paid out to one man the Rev. Thomas Johnson Missionary of the Methodist Episcopal Church," the letter reads, "by means of contract with the Society and a subcontract between the Society and him for the purpose of keeping up an Indian manual labor school among the Shawnees, but instead of performing his duties in a just humane and honorable manner, the Shawnee children when sent to the Mission school complain of insufficient and unpalatable food, of neglect in sickness, and in many instances the children have [died] before the parents were ever informed of their sickness, and so little regard was paid to their health and cleanliness that when brought home the children were in many instances covered with body lice."[25]

Upon encountering Gore that spring morning in 1854, Johnson would have recognized in the aristocrat the familiar air of someone accustomed to being waited on by servants. Johnson was an enslaver and a member of the Kansas legislature, which would later the enact proslavery laws that sparked the Bleeding Kansas violence of the 1850s.[26] In seeing Gore being attended to by servants with powdered hair and knee breeches, Johnson might have thought it would be enriching for his son to experience such a custom. Or he might have just wanted young William to get a free breakfast out of it. Either way, the reverend was evidently comfortable enough with the situation to allow the boy to break bread with Gore.

It's interesting to note that Gore's contact with the enslaving Johnson came not long after Gore did business with another person who was involved in a high-profile slavery issue in St. Louis, John F.A. Sandford, the owner of one of the nation's most famous enslaved people, Dred Scott. Sanford had

Top: Dred Scott. *Bottom*: John F.A. Sanford. *Wikimedia Commons.*

been named as the defendant in Dred Scott's federal lawsuit as Gore was arriving in St. Louis in 1853, a situation Gore might have read about in the local papers. The lawsuit sought thousands of dollars in damages, alleging that Sanford not only illegally held Dred Scott and his wife and children as slaves but had also, in 1853, assaulted and detained the Scotts.

Sanford was a graduate of West Point who rose to the rank of major and became a frontiersman in the West before marrying into the enslaving Chouteau family and expanding the family's merchant banking business to become the Pierre Chouteau Jr. Sanford & Company. Gore did his banking with Pierre Chouteau Jr. Sanford & Company in the spring of 1854; the company cashed drafts for Gore for £300, £700 and £800. Gore likely needed the money for the purposes of paying the forty or so men who accompanied him on his Western safari.[27]

After receiving those funds, Gore left St. Louis and arrived in Westport, in the modern-day Kansas City area, as the Kansas-Nebraska Act was going into effect in May 1854. The first territorial governor's offices were located at Johnson's Shawnee Mission near Gore's camp, and less than a year after Gore departed Westport, the mission became the state capital. From there, Johnson and the legislature promulgated the controversial proslavery laws that brought murder and mayhem into the area. Westport later became the site of the largest Civil War battle west of the Mississippi River.

The South's headquarters during that battle was the house belonging to Thomas Maxwell "Boston" Adams, a plantation owner and Southern sympathizer. In a 1906 *Kansas City Star* story, self-described old-timer Mrs. N.M. Harris described Gore as making fast friends with Adams.

"This nobleman met Mr. Adams and so pleased was he with our neighbor that he spent much of his time with him and took the major as his guest on the hunt," Harris wrote. "The Englishman hadn't one whit the advantage of Mr. Adams either in distinguished appearance, dignified manner or ability to quaff good old English ale."[28]

Adams, Sanford and Reverend Thomas Johnson all met with grim fates not long after meeting Gore.

Adams was arrested and imprisoned in St. Louis during the Civil War, according to Harris's account, and "either died in prison or soon after his release, the result of his confinement when a federal prisoner" on October 22, 1865, at the age of fifty-three.[29]

Sanford suffered a psychotic break after the Dred Scott decision was handed down by the U.S. Supreme Court, even though the court had ruled in his favor and decided against making Scott a free man. The extreme contentiousness of the case had put the country one step closer to war, something Sanford may have been reckoning with, as he was "stricken down with insanity" after the Supreme Court rendered "so wicked and deplorable a decision," *The Chicago Tribune* reported in March 1857. Sanford "recovered his reason after a time, but not permanently; he was again stricken, and died under the infliction" on May 5, 1857, at the age of fifty-one.[30]

If Sanford had mixed feelings about his support of slavery, it couldn't compare to those of the enslaver Reverend Thomas Johnson, who, after being a proslavery advocate and helping usher in the violence in Westport with his vote in favor of slavery, became a Union supporter once the war began. When the group of marauding pro-Confederate guerrillas known as "Bushwhackers" began wreaking havoc in Missouri during the war, Johnson was among their targets. The group attempted to break into his Westport-area home in January 1865, and while he was able to block them from doing so, the Bushwhackers fired a shot through his door that killed him almost instantly. William Johnson was nineteen at the time and, along with his mother and another young man who was staying at the house, defended the property against the group, who fired some fifty shots into the house over the course of an hour and a half before riding away.[31]

4

THE LEGEND OF GORE'S PASS

After leaving the future Civil War battleground of Westport in 1854, Sir St. George Gore soon arrived in the Colorado Territory, ready to hunt big game. His hunt would later be remembered in infamy by historians like Hubert Howe Bancroft, who, in 1890, wrote that Gore's goal in "seeking the mighty solitudes of the heart of the American continent was the gratification of that savage instinct preserved with so much care by the landed aristocracy of Great Britain."[32]

More than 130 years later, Gore is still being criticized. One of the main complaints lodged against Gore today is the fact that he became the namesake of areas he likely didn't visit, like Gore Mountain and Gore Lake in the Gore Range and Gore Creek in Vail, Colorado.

But there's one place in Colorado named after Gore that he did visit, and he made an indelible mark there: Gore Pass at the northern edge of the Gore Range. In a time when roads over mountain passes are commonplace, it's hard to comprehend just how ahead of their time the Gore party was when they created the first wagon road over the mountains in western Colorado.

Before Gore arrived, the pass was just a small footpath traveled by the Ute and Arapahoe tribes, known to few mountain men other than Jim Bridger, who took Gore there. Gore ordered the path to be widened and graded so his wagons could travel it, and western Colorado's first mountain road was built at that moment. Gore was reported to have traveled it with more than a dozen wagons, loaded up with gear like the adventure vans that travel the West today. Gore and his men must have realized they had achieved a feat worthy of recognition, as they left their names carved in a tree atop the pass.

The summit of Gore Pass in Colorado. *Scott Cramer.*

In 1861, Bridger returned to the pass, this time guiding engineer Edward L. Berthoud and Indian Agent Harvie M. Vaile, who were eager to find a stage line from Denver to Salt Lake City following the formation of Colorado as an official territory of the United States. Berthoud's expedition received coverage in the news at the time, with reports saying that one of the new passes discovered on the mission would be called Berthoud Pass. The 1861 coverage also referred to another already-named pass, "Gore's Pass."[33] Vaile, in a report to the territorial governor, said that Bridger had guided Gore through there already "with a train of some 20 wagons, hence we gave it the name of 'Gore's Pass.'"[34]

In 1863, *The Daily Rocky Mountain News* published a report from Major Edward W. Wynkoop, describing an expedition he led over Gore Pass, in which he found "the names of [Gore] and party rudely carved on trees, bearing the date of 1854."[35]

In 1865, General Bela M. Hughes, a pioneer stage manager, opened a route between Denver and Salt Lake City over Gore Pass, "taking advantage of the work already done by Gore," *The Steamboat Pilot* reported some years later.[36]

Hughes said he left Salt Lake City on June 5, 1865, and reached Hot Sulfur Springs in Colorado on September 20, using Gore Pass to make his journey. He wrote an account of his 1865 expedition over Gore Pass for the *Pilot*, which was published in 1902.

Note: The river then referred to as "Bear" is now known as the Yampa River.

> *There was no sign whatever of whites along my route until we reached Empire on Clear creek, and no wagon track until we reached Bear river valley, where we found one of the camps of Sir George Gore, who many years previously, with a large outfit of men and wagons, had penetrated the Beaver river country on a hunting tour through the Rocky Mountains, coming into your country from Ft. Laramie, through Ft. Bridger, and cutting the road out over what is now known as the Gore range. I found many relics of his route and my party followed his track easterly through the famous Gore pass, which is really only a road cut through the timber at the head of what is now called Egeria park.*[37]

A stage company was incorporated to run between the two cities on the route over Gore Pass designated by Hughes, but the company didn't last long. Also at that time, the Pacific Railroad began considering Gore Pass for a route, but that effort didn't last long either.

Major John Wesley Powell, famous for his 1869 study of the Green and Colorado Rivers, in which he made the first recorded descent of the Colorado River through the Grand Canyon, was fond of Gore Pass, using it in both his 1869 expedition and a prior scientific exploration of the Colorado Territory in 1868.

John Wesley Powell (*right*), with Tau-gu of the Southern Paiute tribe, on an 1871–72 expedition of the Colorado River. The photographer is presumed to be Frederick Samuel Dellenbaugh. *Wikimedia Commons*.

The Chicago Tribune, on October 26, 1868, published Ned E. Farrell's account of a side quest he and Powell took to the top of a mountain in the Gore Range while on the 1868 scientific exploration. After climbing the 13,556-foot Gore Range peak that would later be named Mount Powell on September 26, 1868, Ferrell said they "returned in safety in the valley and joined the party at Gore's Pass."[38]

On May 14, 1869, *The Daily Rocky Mountain News* published notes from an unidentified member of Powell's 1869 party, who detailed how the party had once again used the road in their expedition.

"After crossing Gore's Pass we enter an open valley twelve miles long, but quite narrow," the writer said. "The land is good enough, but very deep snows fall."[39]

An oil tanker train travels along the Colorado River near Gore Canyon in Colorado. *John LaConte.*

Around that time, the snow-capped range nearby began receiving the moniker "Gore's Range" in the local media. In 1868, *The Daily Rocky Mountain News* described the view from Long's Peak in Colorado as being "very extensive in all directions; including Pike's Peak, south, the Sahwatch ranges southwest, Gore's range and the Elkhorn Mountains west,"[40] and in 1870, *The Colorado Miner* newspaper described the western and northwestern rim of Middle Park area as "a cluster of snowy peaks belonging to Gore's range of mountains."[41]

In 1877, a proposed Golden, Central and Georgetown railway considered Gore Pass for a route, but like the 1866 railway idea, it never materialized. The notes from the 1877 railway effort make for interesting study today, because even at that early date, the possibility of exporting fossil fuels out of the Uinta Basin on a rail line that ran from Utah to Denver was already showing potential, as was coal mining in the area between Middle Park and the White River. By the 1990s, more than 10 million tons of coal per year was being extracted from mines in the area between Middle Park and the White River,[42] and in 2025, the U.S. Supreme Court ruled in favor of a proposal to extract crude oil out of the Uinta Basin by rail.[43]

An 1877 story in *The Daily Rocky Mountain News* described the proposed Golden, Central and Georgetown railway as running from Denver, over Berthoud Pass into Middle Park, over "Gore's pass or the canon of Grand river" into the White River Valley, to Green River, to the Uinta and Duchene Rivers, to Provo Canyon and eventually to the settlement on the Great Salt Lake in Utah.

"Resources of the country through which the road is projected are various and abundant," the paper reported. "It is claimed from scientific tests that the coals of Middle park, and the coal fields of White river, are of extraordinary value for the manufacture of gas."

Also, "Petroleum springs abound on Uinta river," the paper added.[44]

The effort to create the railroad dragged on throughout the remainder of the nineteenth century. By 1897, Gore Pass had begun to look overgrown, *The Georgetown Courier* reported. While the *Courier* got the year of Gore's expedition wrong (writing 1855 when it had actually occurred in 1854), it nonetheless recognized the significance of the road Gore created.

"In [Gore's] expedition in Western Colorado, he cut a road over the range and lately this road has been discovered," the *Courier* wrote on August 28, 1897. "Although it is entirely overgrown, it can be distinctly traced for several miles by the young trees that make the path. In places the road is cut out and evidences of attempts to grade can be seen and in several places have been found traces of the camp that was there in 1855."[45]

Construction on the Denver and Salt Lake Railway finally began in 1902. The route bypassed Gore Pass, but Gore's name remained linked to the railway nonetheless, as a nearby canyon was being called Gore Canyon, and a route through that canyon was selected. Today, the Gore Canyon portion of the route is considered among the most unique and scenic sections of railroad in Colorado.

The train through Gore Canyon may have created one less reason for people to need to use the Gore Pass wagon road, but not long after, the road received a historic revival with the invention of the automobile. In 1912, *The Steamboat Pilot* published its first account of a motorized trip up Gore Pass, taken by members of the chamber of commerce and the media to raise awareness about the road's potential as an automobile corridor.

"The first settlers used it and it was for many years the principal highway into Northwestern Colorado," the *Pilot* wrote of Gore Pass in 1912. "It then later fell into disuse....The grade, however, is fine and much of the road in splendid shape. It is a beautiful scenic drive and would immediately become a favorite with automobiles if it was put in shape....If the county will do a little work at this time and make the road passable, the state highway commission, as soon as its funds are made available, will expend a great deal of money here, making it the main automobile highway across the northwestern part of the state."[46]

That idea eventually came to fruition eight years later. In May 1920, work was finally started to make Gore Pass a proper automobile road in a state-county collaboration, just like that proposed by the *Pilot*. And once again, the *Pilot* was there to cover the creation of the road and provide a bit of historical background, writing that "the modern automobile will soon be making its way where pioneer hunter and stage driver blazed the trail" in a story from May 19, 1920.

The road "was first crossed with wagons" by Gore, the *Pilot* reported, "in quest of slaughter."[47]

The Daily Rocky Mountain News wrote in 1920 that Gore Pass was "one of the oldest, if not the oldest, wagon roads across the Continental Divide in Colorado," and "before the season is over, the sound of the automobile will be heard for the first time on the pass by which white men first entered the great country of northwest Colorado."[48]

In 1876, writer George Heldt published an account of Gore's expedition from Henry Bostwick, who was among Gore's retinue. Heldt said Gore was a Napoleon-like figure to the men of his expedition,[49] a description the German philosopher Georg Wilhelm Friedrich Hegel might have appreciated, as both Gore and Napoleon had the ability to "reach out over the world and master it," in Hegel's words, a description that led to Napoleon receiving the moniker of "history on horseback."

If Napoleon was history on horseback, Gore then, in the American West, was wreckreation on vacation. Like Napoleon, Gore also bent the arc of history as he traveled, leaving behind the roads that opened up a new era of exploration in the West. But unlike Napoleon, Gore did this for the purposes of seeking recreation, more specifically "recreation that wrecks or harms the environment," to borrow the definition of *wreckreation* from Wiktionary.org.

Gore's Pass was such a notable road in western Colorado, it wasn't long before the name Gore's Range was ascribed to the nearby mountain range that the pass skirts around to the north. And once it became the Gore Range, Gore Canyon became the obvious name for the gorge coming out of it and Gore Lake the obvious name for a prominent lake in the range. The Gore Lake Trail will get you there, and Gore Creek exits the lake and flows into the Gore Valley, where homes dot Gore Circle and the iconic

Colorado Highway 134, otherwise known as Gore Pass. *Scott Cramer.*

view of the Gore Range from Gore Creek Drive appears on postcards sent around the world.

The fact that all these names sprang from the creation of Gore Pass is further evidence of how significant a road it is and what it represents. Gore wasn't just a hunter; he was also a trailblazer, allowing others to follow in his tracks. The road's status as "the pass by which white men first entered the great country of northwest Colorado" is what kept Gore in the minds of Coloradans for decades following his visit, and while his name is now most commonly associated with the Gore Range and Gore Creek in Vail, Colorado, it was Gore Pass that made Sir St. George Gore a legend.

5

COURSING THROUGH THE FAMINE

Seventy years after Gore's journey through Colorado, his travels were proclaimed to be "probably the most elaborate, expensive and largest hunting caravan on record which ever penetrated the Rockies," a claim that went unquestioned.[50]

But what has been questioned is how Gore was able to undertake such a journey—how could he afford such an expensive and long-lasting vacation in the Rockies?

The answer lies in the lucky happenstance of his birth on April 28, 1811, in Dublin, Ireland. Gore was the youngest child and only son of Grace and Ralph Gore; in 1802, Ralph had become a baronet, the owner of a vast, private landholding, after the death of his uncle, also named Ralph Gore (but better known as the First Earl of Ross), who divided up his inheritance among his three nephews, one of whom was Ralph, Sir St. George Gore's father.[51]

When Ralph died in England in 1842, his son, St. George, became the eighth baronet of the Gore Baronetcy of Magherabegg in the County of Donegal in Ireland. He became a wreckreation-on-vacation figure almost immediately, using the wealth of the Gore Baronetcy to help bring about an evolution in British hunting and fishing.

The Gore Baronetcy is an excellent example of what resulted from the so-called Protestant Ascendancy, as the baronetcy was formed just as the large-scale colonization of Ireland was giving birth to the Ascendancy class in the seventeenth century. The English occupation in Ireland was a

Hounds chase a hare at the Waterloo Cup in 1921. *Smith Archive/Alamy stock photo.*

centuries-long process, beginning with the Anglo-Norman invasions of the late twelfth century, but that occupation became more widespread starting in the sixteenth century as the Reformation took hold in England. Amid this period of religious and political transformation, families like the Gores would rise after demonstrating their loyalty to the Crown.

The Reformation, which saw England break from the Catholic Church and embrace Protestantism in the 1500s, created a new justification for the Crown to take control of its Catholic adversaries in Ireland. The religious divide fueled efforts from England to dominate the island, especially in the northern province of Ulster, which had been free from English rule. In 1594, the Nine Years' War broke out as Irish chieftains fought back against English occupation in Ulster, which is where the Gore Baronetcy traces its origins. More specifically, the Gore family's fortunes were the indirect result of a moment of crisis for the English: the Battle of the Yellow Ford in 1598. Fought on the River Blackwater near Armagh, the battle saw Irish forces inflict a major defeat on an English column.

In response to this setback, the Crown dispatched reinforcements to reassert control in Ulster. Among them was Paul Gore, born in London in 1567, who arrived as commander of a cavalry troop. He remained in service to the Crown for the remainder of the war and, following its conclusion in 1603, was rewarded with 1,348 acres of confiscated land in the Ulster county of Donegal, formally designated Manor Gore. In true Ascendancy fashion, the family then parlayed this initial grant into a lasting legacy over time, encompassing more than 150,000 acres by the late nineteenth century.

The Echo newspaper in London, in 1879, ran a column about how the Gores were able to accomplish this, summarizing the family's rise in the Peerage of Ireland with a humorous stanza from Thomas Moore's 1819 poem "New Creation of Peers":

> *Tis pleasant—while nothing but mercantile fractures,*
> *Some simple, some compound, is dinned in our ears—*
> *To think that, tho' robbed all coarse manufactures,*
> *We still have our fine manufacture of Peers*

The poem pokes fun at how, despite the economic problems being fretted over in Ireland at the time, the Anglo-Irish aristocracy was undeterred in its ability to create or "manufacture" new nobility (peers).

The Gore coat of arms. *Wikimedia Commons.*

While Paul Gore didn't quite make it to the peerage, he did become an official baronet in the Baronetage of Ireland in 1622 before his death in 1629. The baronetcy was then passed on to his eldest son, Ralph, while his second son, Arthur, "obtained a grant of the lands of Newtown, in Mayo, created into the Manor of Castle Gore in 1666," the *Echo* reported. "Henceforth the various branches of the family pursued a quiet and inglorious course of self-aggrandisement, marrying heiresses whenever they had the opportunity, and securing for their younger sons a share in the Church's feast of fat things.…It is hardly necessary to say that these enormous possessions were chiefly derived through confiscations."[52]

As the Gore family was manufacturing new peers, the British Empire was expanding around the globe, laying claim to the rest of Ireland and establishing colonies in the Americas. It may not have been apparent at the time, but it is now widely accepted that England's learnings in conquering Ireland in the sixteenth century influenced the strategies it later adopted in colonizing the Americas. From the textbook *America, Past and Present*:

> *Before they crossed the Atlantic, English settlers moved to Ireland. Their experiences there powerfully shaped how later migrants would view the New World. It was on this island that enterprising Englishmen first learned to subdue a foreign population and to seize its lands.*[53]

Fast forward to the British tourists who became fascinated with the western United States in the mid-nineteenth century, and we find a strong connection between both projects. Our protagonist Sir St. George Gore is an excellent example, being raised in the British Empire's colony of Ireland and using the spoils gained there to witness the colonization of America taking place in real time. The connection is most symbolic during Gore's visit with the Reverend Thomas Johnson at the Shawnee boarding school grounds in 1854, as the Native boarding schools in the United States and the British-formed schools in Ireland contained many commonalities, and Gore had at least one of those schools on his lands.

In the 1730s, a letter from the Protestant archbishop of Armagh resulted in the formation of a crown charter from the British government to create public schools in Ireland. The letter expressed a desire to educate the people of the Irish frontier, saying that "in many parts of the kingdom there are great tracts of mountainy and coarse lands of ten, twenty or thirty miles in length and of a considerable breadth, almost universally inhabited by papists," and the formation of public schools could be used "for converting and civilizing these poor deluded people, and bringing them, in time, to be good Christians and faithful subjects."

It's similar language to that used by the U.S. Congress in the Civilization Fund Act of 1819, which referenced "the further decline and final extinction of the Indian tribes, adjoining the frontier settlements of the United States," and sought to introduce, among those tribes, "the habits and arts of civilization."

Both the British Crown's Charter of 1733 and the U.S. Civilization Fund Act of 1819 resulted in the creation of systems that would administer federal funding to such schools. In Ireland, "in order to perform more efficiently the task of proselytizing the popish Irish, the society created a number of boarding schools, thus allowing it to remove children entirely from parental influence," wrote Donald H. Akenson in *The Irish Education Experiment: The National System of Education in the Nineteenth Century.* At these boarding schools, one of the striking features, Akenson wrote, "was the amount of manual labor performed by the children...garden and farm labor occupied the boys, spinning and cloth manufacture the girls."[54]

Similarly, at the Native boarding schools of the United States, one of the goals, according to the language in the Civilization Fund Act of 1819, was to "instruct [students] in the mode of agriculture suited to their situation."

At the schools in Ireland, a backlash began as abuses were documented,[55] and by the time a school was formed on Gore's property in the 1840s, the comparatively liberal Whig Party had set up a new national school system that was more sympathetic to the desires of the Irish Catholics regarding education. A new National Board of Education was created in 1831, and while it aimed to create nonreligious institutions, there was pushback from Anglo-Irish Protestants who abhorred the board's decision to disallow Bible studies during school hours. A watering down of the board's nonreligious doctrines began almost immediately, and the culture of the schools became more British than Irish, giving way to the formation of similar institutions in England that used the same textbooks. As a result, "it becomes clear that the common peasant would have no voice at all in deciding how his children were to be taught," Akenson wrote. "Ultimately, the only way a parent could express disapproval of the conduct of his local national school was to withdraw his child from education."[56]

That appears to be what happened at Gore's school in King's County, Ireland. The school "was opened and placed under the National Board of Education; but as the master appointed was a Protestant, it is stated that the children were all withdrawn from the school and consequently it was closed," according to an 1849 newspaper report.[57]

It's unclear how involved Gore was in the activities taking place on his holdings, but if he had at least a cursory briefing of the efforts to set up a school on his land in King's County, then the experience would have lent itself to an interesting conversation between Johnson and Gore in Kansas. While Johnson might have viewed his boarding school as a novel idea, to Gore, it likely would have been seen as a standard tool deployed from the colonizer's cabinet, one that is wielded easily in theory but becomes more difficult to handle in practice.

Like history on horseback (or wreckreation on vacation), the glamorous camping party on Johnson's property being undertaken by Gore, who was enjoying a holiday paid for by his plantations in Ireland, was the future roaring ahead, drowning out the echoes of the past that could still be heard reverberating off the walls of the nearby boarding school. And the fact that Gore was there to kill bison makes his caricature of a history-on-horseback figure even more on the nose. A British modus operandi in Ireland, at one time, had been to clear the forests of the trees which the native Irish used as cover while attacking the Normans. These clearings also conveniently doubled as newly formed grazing grounds on which the Crown could maximize its profitable exports of cattle. In the United States, Gore is an unwitting agent of history in that regard also, as the removal of bison—the primary food source for many Native tribes—was encouraged by the U.S. military in an effort to clear the lands for incoming settlers and cattle.

In 1872, another Irish-born traveler to the Great Plains, British army Officer Sir William Francis Butler, published a memoir of his travels to the American West and Canada, lamenting the loss of the region's Native cultures and the bison on which they depended.

"My God, what a terrible tale could I not tell of these dark deeds done by the white savage against the far nobler red man," Butler wrote. "'Kill every buffalo you see,' said a Yankee colonel to me one day in Nebraska; 'every buffalo dead is an Indian gone.'"[58]

John R. Cook, who was stationed in the Indian Territory along the Kansas-Missouri border during the American Civil War, published a memoir in 1907 in which he quoted one of the United States' most famous generals telling the Texas legislature something similar in 1875:

> *General Phil. Sheridan was then in command of the military department of the Southwest, with headquarters at San Antonio. When he heard of the nature of the Texas bill for the protection of the buffaloes, he went to Austin, and, appearing before the joint assembly of the House and Senate, so the story goes, told them that they were making a sentimental mistake by legislating in the interest of the buffalo. He told them that instead of stopping the hunters they ought to give them a hearty, unanimous vote of thanks, and appropriate a sufficient sum of money to strike and present to each one a medal of bronze, with a dead buffalo on one side and a discouraged Indian on the other. He said: "These men have done in the last two years and will do more in the next year, to settle the vexed Indian question, than the entire regular army has done in the last thirty years. They are destroying the Indians' commissary; and it is a well-known fact that an army losing its base of supplies is placed at a great disadvantage. Send them powder and lead, if you will; but, for the sake of a lasting peace, let*

> *them kill, skin, and sell until the buffaloes are exterminated. Then your prairies can be covered with speckled cattle, and the festive cowboy, who follows the hunter as a second forerunner of an advanced civilization.*"[59]

Gore, then, in killing thousands of bison while also building roads in his path, could be seen to be "anointed by the invisible hand of History to execute the task necessary to usher in a new age of human civilization," as the history-on-horseback description of Napoleon has been explained.[60] And Gore to recreation, like Napoleon to revolution, seemed to engage in this wherever he went, starting not long after he took his title of baronet in 1842.

Just two years after taking his title, Gore was already being credited with bringing a new style of hunting to Scotland. The *Inverness Courier*, in March 1844, reported on a pair of local men (whom the newspaper called, simply, Mr. White and Mr. Rose) trying out a method of waterfowl hunting using an extremely large shotgun known as a punt gun. The punt gun, a cartoonish-looking weapon that's twice the size of an average man, was mounted to a boat and could kill fifty ducks in a single shot. An enormous weapon of English design, it had never been seen in the Scottish Highlands before Gore brought one there.

"The exciting sport of winter shooting on a large scale was first introduced in this quarter by Sir St. George Gore, Bart. [an abbreviation for baronet], who sent down his complete apparatus, constructed after the most approved method, as used on the coast of England," the *Courier* reported."[61]

Later, Gore was remembered by the *Courier* as the man who "introduced punt shooting in the North, and was also the first to use a particular kind of Irish fishingrod on the Ness," which later became the preferred implement among anglers there.[62]

In *Baronet in an Earth Lodge*, author Barry C. Johnson examined the lands and titles Gore received in Ireland in 1842, but the period between Gore inheriting the baronetcy in 1842 and the first previously known mention of Gore in America in 1854 was left unexplained. If that created a question in the reader's mind about how Gore was occupying his time in those years, the answer is—you guessed it—hunting and fishing. And as it turns out, long before Gore became famous in the United States for the thousands of animals he killed, he was already somewhat of a celebrity sportsman in the United Kingdom. I've discovered reports of Gore killing more than two thousand animals in Scotland before he reached North America, culminating with a hunt during the 1847 season, which was described by

Waterfowl hunter Snowden Slights displays a punt gun, circa 1900–12. *Sydney Harold Smith, Library of Congress.*

one reporter as "the most extraordinary exploit recorded in the history of venatic sports."

It's unclear how and when Gore became so passionate about his sporting pursuits. He attended secondary school at Winchester in England and was an undergraduate student at Oriel College in Oxford until 1834, at which point he ended his formal education without earning a degree. Johnson, in *Baronet in an Earth Lodge*, wrote that it was not surprising that Gore finished school "without bothering the examiners at all," because "with no living to earn, why should he need a degree?"

"Like many young men of his class and day," Johnson added, "he was no doubt at Oxford for social rather than for educational reasons."[63]

Gore had apparently become friendly with the Craven family, of the famed "Craven Stakes" horse races, and was with a member of that family in Ireland in 1837 when tragedy struck. The friends were in the area known as the Leap of Doonass, better known as the Falls of Doonass, a famous fishing spot that no longer exists following the diversion of the River

A punt gun mounted to a punt boat. *Sydney Harold Smith, Wikimedia Commons.*

Shannon in the 1920s. The falls were located on the narrowest portion of the Shannon, where it descended more than fifty vertical feet in half a mile, forcing boaters to exit their crafts upstream and ford the river on foot.[64]

Gore is only tangentially involved in the events that cost his friend his life at the falls, but it's worth recounting the whole story to get an understanding of the lessons he likely learned from the incident, including a respect for the power of nature and the importance of trusting local guides.

From the *Limerick Chronicle*'s April 5, 1837 edition:

> *Mr. Craven, son of Mr. Fuller Craven, of Gloucester, a young gentleman of fortune, and highly connected in England, was trout fishing above the Leap of Doonas yesterday, with his servant, when both were doomed to find a premature grave. He had been on a visit some time to Mr. St. George Gore, son of Sir Ralph Gore, of Brighton, at a handsome sporting lodge, commanding the romantic scenery of Doonas and Castle Connell, where both friends enjoyed peculiar facilities for fishing. Between five and six last evening, a girl from Doonas, who had letters for Caastle Connell post-office, got a seat in the cot which carried Mr. Craven and his servant, and she*

> *took the paddle to ferry them across the river, but Mr. Craven not liking the way the frail bark was making, took the paddle from the girl and said he would save her the trouble of guiding its course. She reluctantly yielded, for it appears the young woman was more expert at managing the cot than Mr. Craven, and acquainted with the river. He unfortunately persevered, and the cot veered round towards the fall of the Leap, and was running fast towards the rapids, when Mr. Craven lost his self-possession, and jumped out to gain a rock within a length of him, but did not succeed, and he sank in a part of the river over the Leap, called the dancing hold, from which he was never more seen to rise. The cot was dashed with violence against another rock, where she split, and his servant also sunk, but the girl clung with desperate tenacity to the remains of the cot, and was taken up below the fall in a state almost lifeless. The fisherman have been since dragging the river for the body of Mr. Craven, but without success.*[65]

It's easy to assume Gore received his love of hunting and fishing from his father, as many boys do, but aside from attending the occasional coursing event in England in the 1830s, Sir Ralph Gore is not mentioned as participating in any sporting activities, which were widely covered in UK newspapers at the time. Young St. George, on the other hand, was already receiving coverage in his twenties, starting with the busy 1840 hunting season in the Scottish Highlands.

"Many gentlemen have returned south after travelling the whole of the north in search of shooting quarters, without being able to obtain a nook or cranny," *The Inverness Courier* reported.[66]

Gore was not one of those unlucky gentlemen. He had secured himself a lodge at Gairloch, and although he was not yet a well-known sportsman in 1840, he was one of the only people noted in the *Courier*'s coverage.

"On the day of his arrival [Gore] killed a noble stag; next day a host of salmon and grilse on the river Ewe (one of 22 lbs); and two days afterwards he killed two stags, right and left, in the forest of Glasletter," the *Courier* reported.[67]

The following year, in 1841, hunting lodges were again in high demand.

"One moor in this neighbourhood, for example, which last year let for £100, has this season brought £150, and numerous applications have been made too late," the *Courier* noted.[68]

Gore secured a property at the Flowerdale House in the Gairloch area of Scotland for the 1841 season and was later reported to have killed five stags "along with great numbers" of grouse, while also catching 152 salmon and grilse.[69]

The Flowerdale House in Scotland, circa 1890–1900. *High Life Highland.*

Gore's father, Sir Ralph, died the following spring at the age of eighty-three, willing all his lands and titles to his son. Gore would have been expected to carry on the family tradition of marrying into another wealthy Ascendancy-class family and protecting his lands and wealth for future generations, but instead of spending his time courting women and attending cocktail parties, Gore seemed to prefer the company of men and the outdoors. While we don't know if Gore received his love of hunting and fishing from his father, we do know for certain he received through his father's death the means to pursue his trophy hunting ambitions on a much grander scale.[70]

Gore's first newsworthy act as baronet occurred less than two months after his father's March 25, 1842 death, appearing at what *The Derby Mercury* called "a numerous and highly respectable assemblage of sporting noblemen and gentlemen." The sportsmen were visiting Hopton Hall in England for "an extraordinary sale of sporting dogs," according to the *Mercury*, and several distinguished guests were in attendance, including Lord Henry Reynolds-Moreton, heir to the Earl of Ducie.[71]

The *Mercury* couldn't have been more apt in that first description of Gore as a baronet. He had become a player in the theater of English gentility, taking seriously his performance in the roles of leisure and recreation. From that moment forward, when Gore was not hunting and fishing, he would be spending time with those highly respectable assemblages of sporting noblemen and gentlemen.

Gore purchased four deerhounds for seventy-five pounds at the May 1842 event, and by July, he had rented out the Flowerdale House in Scotland again, "where he has one of the best shootings and fishings in the North," *The Caledonian Mercury* reported.[72] A month later, Gore was back in the papers, which reported that in an eight-day period in the River Ewe, he had caught sixty-two salmon, one of which weighed thirty pounds.[73] In October, *The Caledonian Mercury* reported on what it called "the feats of that noble sport, deer stalking," saying Gore killed twenty-two male and six female deer, "along with some roe deer" in Gairloch.

"At Pock-a-Buy lodge, Sir St. George Gore killed eleven stags in eight days—four of them in one day, and three of them at one stalking," the *Mercury* reported.[74]

Gore returned to the Scottish moors the following season, where he was reported to have killed "two fine stags, one of them with eleven points" in August 1843.[75] In September, he was hunting in the Kinlochewe area, where the *Mercury* reported that Gore had "a fortunate day of deer stalking on the

Hunters stalk the Scottish Highlands, circa 1880–90. *High Life Highland.*

19th, having secured three stags, two of them with royal heads," adding that "one of these is the finest we have seen this season, the top of each beam is surmounted with a formidable triangle of antlers."[76]

In 1844, Gore rented out the massive Inverbroom estate in the northwest highlands of Scotland, where he was recorded as killing 82 brace (a term for pairs) of grouse and 4 stags in mid-August[77] and 376 brace of grouse and 8 hares over a five-day period at the end of August.[78] The following month, Gore was reported to have shot "five stags, two of them very heavy, and with large heads of horns, one set of antlers 30 inches in length."[79]

In 1845, Gore was again at Inverbroom, where he started off the summer with some salmon fishing in July.[80] A month later, he was killing grouse by the hundreds after moving down to the Strathvaich Lodge, where, on August 23, he killed 130 grouse, "and on the 25th an equal number, two snipe, and two hares," *The Inverness Courier* reported. "Sir St. George had also a double shot at two fine stags, killing both, right and left."[81] Moving south to the Achindarroch area in September, Gore was reported to have killed another 317 animals, including grouse and hare.[82]

If it sounds like Gore was doing an insane amount of killing, it could be because he had become determined to stand out among that highly respectable assemblage of sporting noblemen and gentlemen. London-based social historian Peter Pagnamenta wrote about Gore in his 2012 book *Prairie Fever: British Aristocrats in the American West*, describing the Scottish hunting season as "both a social ritual and a contest in culling" and writing that Gore was among the most competitive participants.[83]

In researching Gore, I often found articles mentioning another member of the respectable assemblage, a man simply referred to as "Mr. Winsloe," who was a local in Coulnakyle, near the area known today as Nethy Bridge in the Scottish Highlands. In September 1843, when Gore was reported to have killed the finest stag of the season, Mr. Winsloe was also in the newspaper for killing 1,714 grouse.[84] August 12 is the first day of grouse hunting season each year in the United Kingdom, an auspicious date still known today as the Glorious Twelfth, and in 1844, the newspapers on that day sought out the expertise of the venerated local Mr. Winsloe to see how the start of the season was faring.

"Mr. Winsloe found the birds very wild and difficult to approach," *The Ross-shire Advertiser* reported. Nevertheless, Mr. Winsloe killed 194 grouse on the Glorious Twelfth, "and on the second day he bagged 77 brace before one-o'clock."[85] In August 1845, Mr. Winsloe killed 568 grouse in six days,[86] and a month later, as Gore made the news for killing "a very

The Inverbroom House in Scotland, circa 1890–1900. *High Life Highland.*

large, fat stag" on September 18, in that same story, we see "Mr. Winsloe bagged 2,500 brace [of grouse]—the greatest number we have heard," the *Advertiser* reported.[87]

In November 1845, "the weather was unfavorable, but this did not in the least damp the ardour of our sportsmen," *The Edinburgh Post* reported, "and in eight successive days, at Inverbroom, Sir St. George Gore, Bart., bagged to his own gun two hundred brace of grouse. On one rough and stormy day he killed thirty-one and a half brace, a hare and a snipe."[88]

Gore closed his 1845 hunting season in December at Inverbroom, where he "had excellent sport on the moors; and from the deer forest he shot 15 stags and 11 roe deer," *The Inverness Courier* reported.[89]

In 1846, Gore was again gracing the pages of the *Courier*, which reported that he killed two deer to start the season in early August.[90] By the middle of the month, Gore was leading the *Courier*'s hunting coverage. From a mid-August 1846 report:

> *Aided by a continuance of the most favourable weather, sportsmen on the moors and in the forests are now in full activity. At Strathvaich, Sir St. George Gore, Bart., began with great success, bagging on the 17th, 77 brace of grouse, 13 hares, and 2 snipes; on the 18th, 76 brace of grouse, 1 woodcock, and 3 hares. On the 19th, he went in pursuit of red deer, and ended a successful stalk by capturing three at once. Later in the day another was*

> *shot; and on the following day a very large fat stag, with ten points on wide branching horns, fell to his rifle.*[91]

A week later, "Sir St. George Gore, Bart., continues to get excellent shooting," the *Courier* reported. "On the 22nd he shot 64 brace of grouse and 13 hares—on the 24th, 90½ brace, a snipe, and 6 hares—on the 26th, a double shot at stags, killing both; and on the 27th, 81½ brace of grouse and 6 hares."[92]

On September 5, 1846, Gore "captured near Inverbroom the largest and finest stag ever seen on the grounds," the *Courier* reported. This was followed up by Gore killing "90 brace of game, a snipe and two hares, and on the 7th, 76½ brace of grouse and five hares."[93]

In October 1846, the *Courier* reported that Gore "stalked and shot five stags last week at Strathvaich—three of them in one day."[94] By November, Gore had killed a total of twenty-seven red deer and four roe deer that fall, including "a stag with the largest head of horns that has been sent for preservation this season," the *Courier* reported. "The length of the beams of the horns, measured along their curves, is thirty-two inches; span at the greatest width of the bow, thirty inches, and armed with thirteen sharp-pointed antlers."[95]

Gore returned to the Scottish Highlands in 1847, renting out the Flowerburn House in early August, where he "killed three good stags on his first day's stalking—two of them with double shots," the *Courier* reported.[96] On the Glorious Twelfth, Gore was back at his favorite hunting lodge at Inverbroom, killing 124 grouse, 5 hares, 3 ducks and 1 woodcock.[97] Repeating his pattern of moving from Inverbroom to Strathvaich, Gore completed what was dubbed by *The Leicestershire Mercury* as "the most extraordinary exploit recorded in the history of venatic sports" when he shot 6 stags in a single stalking.[98] *The Aberdeen Journal* covered the event as well:

> *DEER STALKING—Now that the season of this sport, which combines the greatest excitement, skill, and perseverance of sportsmen, draws towards its termination, every effort is made to add to the list of the antlered trophies, to adorn the hall or shooting lodge. Last week has been a most successful one. In the forests near Strathvaich, Sir St. George Gore, Bart., had three days of great success, as during that time 13 deer were stalked and shot—6 of them in one day, at one stalking. Six barrels were fired in succession, and four out of the six laid each a fine deer dead on the spot; the other, severely wounded, gave a short run to the deer hounds, who quickly brought them to bay.*[99]

The Flowerburn House in Scotland, circa 1901–14. *High Life Highland.*

In 1848, Gore shifted his focus away from hunting and toward the emerging sport of coursing, in which two greyhounds compete to see which can catch a hare first using sight rather than scent. While the sport had been in practice since the mid-seventeenth century, in the 1830s, it started to become a sporting institution in England with the advent of a competition known as the Waterloo Cup. In 1836, the cup attracted eight competitors; sixteen sportsmen competed the following year, and it was doubled again to host thirty-two competitors the year after that. For the next 167 years, the Waterloo Cup continued to run, attracting tens of thousands of spectators and gamblers each season until its final event in 2005.[100]

Gore had appeared in his first coursing event in 1847, immediately taking to it. In 1848, he put his deerhounds up for sale and announced he would not be heading to Scotland that season; instead, he would be focusing on coursing.[101] Later that year, his hound "Cytherea" won the Craven Puppy Stakes coursing event. His hound "Magician" won the cup at the Ashdown Park Coursing Competition, his hound "Queen Mab" won the Chippenham Stakes for Puppies at the Newmarket Champion Coursing Meeting and his hound "Shade" bested thirty-one other dogs to win the Waterloo Cup.[102]

The news that Gore was no longer hunting in the forests of Scotland may have come as welcome news to those who would compete against him each season for the most game killed. The 1849 hunting season was one of the best on record for Mr. Winsloe, who killed 1,642 grouse, 303 partridges, 155 hares, 75 rabbits, 61 snipe, 48 woodcocks, 41 blackcocks, 21 wild ducks, 17 golden plovers, 17 roe deer, 9 teal, 4 foxes and 1 pheasant for a total of 2,394 animals killed in a single season.

Meanwhile, Gore won the Waterloo Cup again in 1849, becoming the first person to win the event in back-to-back years. His success caught the eye of *The Glasgow Daily Mail* in its coverage of the cup, which, by that point, was regarded as the "Blue Ribbon of the Leash," the largest coursing event in the world.

"It is remarkable that Sir St. George Gore, who has but recently commenced coursing, has won the cup two years in succession," *The Daily Mail* reported.

Between the moors of Scotland and the Waterloo Cup in England, it's obvious that the life of a traveling sportsman was Gore's primary pastime in the 1840s. But while Gore was receiving news coverage of his exploits, his

Violence breaks out in Ireland during the Great Famine, as depicted in *The Pictorial Times* in 1846. *Wikimedia Commons.*

native Ireland was making headlines for what would be regarded as the most tragic and infuriating period in its history—the Great Famine, in which an estimated one million people died of starvation while massive amounts of food were exported from the country.

Irish historian Helen Litton researched journals, government documents, newspaper articles and artwork to assemble a straightforward history of the famine in her book *The Irish Famine: An Illustrated History*. The book is not for the faint of heart. As Gore and Mr. Winsloe killed enough game to feed entire villages in 1846, newspapers were publishing horrific accounts of starvation and death, which Litton chronicled in her book.

"One writer described the inquest on a father of two very young children," Litton wrote. "His death had only been discovered when the children toddled into Schull, crying with hunger, and complaining that their father would not talk to them. The same writer viewed the body of a woman called Kate Barry, buried so lightly that she had been uncovered by dogs, and partially eaten. He thought he saw part of a horse's tail lying nearby, but discovered it was the skin and hair of her scalp. Thirty yards away, two wretched houses contained four dead bodies; although they had been dead a fortnight, they had not yet been buried."[103]

The Ascendancy class owned most of the land and had almost limitless power over their tenants, Litton wrote.

"Many of these landlords lived in England and were called 'absentees,'" Litton wrote. "They used land agents to administer their property, and most of them had no interest in it except to spend the money the rents brought in."[104]

Gore fit the description of an absentee landlord all too well, hunting in Scotland and coursing in England while the famine ravaged his lands in Ireland. His immediate family emigrated from Ireland back to England sometime in the 1820s, when Gore was in college, with little evidence of much time spent in Ireland after that. The family sought out the fashionable resort town of Brighton in England, where Gore's parents and two of his three older sisters, Grace, Martha Elizabeth and Elizabeth Esther, lived the rest of their lives. Gore's father died in Brighton in 1842, leaving his lands and tenants to Gore just a few years before the outbreak of famine.

Litton detailed the results of an 1840s-era English study known as the Devon Commission, which determined that the land system and landlords like Gore were to blame for the widespread poverty in Ireland. But the British system of laissez-faire (meaning "let be") capitalism also played a major role. Laissez-faire capitalism was the dominant economic theory at the time, something that "has to be remembered, because otherwise a lot of the Government's attitudes to the disaster in Ireland do not make sense," Litton wrote.[105]

The system only worked because Irish tenants working for landlords like Gore had a food source that could be grown easily with little labor required: the potato. When the potato crop began to fail in 1845 due to a fungal disease known as "blight," people starved, and the laissez-faire capitalist system started breaking down. Landlords were still responsible for payments to the British government for every tenant on their lands, regardless of whether those tenants could pay rent to their landlords. Eventually, landlords like Gore, who were facing bills themselves, were no longer able to collect rent from their tenants; therefore, "the only way to collect enough money was to clear the poor from their small plots, and to relet the land in bigger lots to people with more money," Litton wrote.

Mass evictions ensued, and the newspapers reported that the tenants who were kicked off their lands were forming secret juries or "vehmgericht" courts aimed at taking revenge through murder.[106] In October 1849, Gore's agent, forty-year-old Charles Trench Cage, was shot and killed after attempting to evict tenants off Gore's land. The news was so widespread it even reached the United States, with *The Daily Republic* newspaper in Washington, D.C., reporting on the incident:

> *Although we have no positive assurance of the details, there was no doubt a secret jury impanelled to decide up on the guilt of the agent, and a court formed to award fitting punishment to the offended against the doctrines of the Irish Vehmgericht. By this fantastic tribunal the unfortunate agent of Sir George Gore was found guilty, and sentence of death passed against him in due form of law. Suitable executioners were selected from the ranks of the secret brotherhood to carry out the doom of the Court, and without a murmur or remonstrance they proceeded to their work.*[107]

In the Parish of Wherry, Gore owned roughly 1,100 acres comprising two townlands, Endrim and Cretan, which were being managed by Cage. At about 10:30 a.m. on Sunday, October 14, 1849, Cage was on his way to church on horseback when his body was "literally riddled on the left side with slugs and bullets," the *Republic* reported. "The collar of the coat and neckcloth were blown off, and the neck alone pierced by five bullets."[108]

The Kings County Chronicle reported that Cage was obliged to carry out the evictions that led to his assassination. It is not known—or not revealed—whether this obligation was of his own design or if it came from Gore, but *The Evening Packet* newspaper suspected the latter, writing that Cage was murdered "because he did his duty towards his employer."[109]

The Kings County Chronicle reported that Cage had been warned prior to the attack.

"Twelve months ago he was obliged to dispossess several tenants; and on the first of the present month four families were evicted, some of whom were admitted into their houses, but they did not get back the land which they had held," the *Chronicle* wrote. "It is reported that it was in contemplation to have several more of the tenants evicted....A person named Molloy was formerly the bailiff on the estate. He was threatened and told that if Mr. Cage came there to reside he would be murdered."[110]

An investigation ensued, and three men, Bernard Gunning, Patrick Kelly and Edward Farrell, were charged with murder. Gore came back to Ireland for the men's initial appearance in court in November 1849,[111] but he didn't stay long, returning to England in early December and swooping up a win at the Ashdown Park Coursing Meet.[112]

Gore continued coursing throughout 1850, winning the February 6–7 Ashdown Park Meeting with his dog "Hermione" and placing runner-up in several other events throughout the year.[113] He probably carried out more evictions that year as well—an October 1850 advertisement announcing he would like to rent out three hundred to five hundred acres of his land in Limerick was the type of advertisement one might run after removing tenants from the property—but none were met with the violence and publicity of Cage's murder.

Gore was named a steward of the Waterloo Cup in March 1851, and later that month, he put his greyhounds up for sale, saying that he was giving up coursing.[114] There was no explanation about why he chose to quit, but it's likely he had started planning his North American adventure at that point. He was reported to have competed in only one event in 1852, the Druid Cup at the Wiltshire Champion Coursing Meeting in October 1852, and he doesn't appear to have participated in any hunts that year. The next time Gore was mentioned in a newspaper, the *Ottawa Daily Citizen* reported his arrival into Canada on the *Lady Eglinton* in July 1853.[115]

While previous writers assumed that Gore began his North American sojourn by arriving in New York or New Orleans, his decision to arrive through the British colony of Canada, then known as British North America, might have been a better assumption, considering how much family Gore had there. Several areas of Canada are named after his fellow descendants of Paul Gore, including the Gore township in Quebec and the municipality of Gore in Nova Scotia.

The Ottawa Citizen, in 1925, traced the Gore family's history in Canada, dating to the 1820s with the arrival of Sir Charles Stephen Gore, better known as Colonel Gore, who was a relative of our Sir St. George Gore and fought in the Lower Canada Rebellion in the 1830s.

"Colonel Gore was the personal friend of the famous Duke of Wellington and placed the first sword in His Grace's hands when he obtained a commission in the 33rd Regiment, which was raised by the colonel's grandfather," the *Citizen* reported. "Col. Gore came out to Canada with his family by the advice of his brother, Admiral John Gore, K.C.B., in 1821, in charge of the ordinance department, conferred on him by the Duke of Wellington through whose influence his second son, Lieut. Col. Gore, in the Royal Artillery, was well-known in Canada during the Fenian invasion in command of a crack battery of artillery."[116]

When our Sir St. George Gore arrived in Canada in 1853, he would have had a cousin, Mary Pitt Gore, living in Montreal at the time, and as Montreal was Gore's final destination aboard the *Lady Eglinton*, it's possible that he chose that route with a visit to her in mind.

6

WRECKREATION ON VACATION

After Gore arrived in Canada in the summer of 1853, he hunted and fished in the Great Lakes region before traveling across the United States from north to south, with a stopover in St. Louis. He then returned to Missouri during the spring of 1854, which is where his story of wreckreation on vacation, which made him a legend in Colorado and the Rocky Mountain West, first begins. While there are a few government reports and newspaper articles that help piece together where Gore may have traveled and when, most of the details of his hunt can be traced to three sources:

- A dispatch from Randolph B. Marcy, an army captain who met Gore in 1857 and wrote about the safari in his 1866 book *Thirty Years of Army Life on the Border.*
- A story from the army's Lieutenant James H. Bradley, who wrote about Gore's expedition in his journal in the 1870s after meeting Henry S. Bostwick, who accompanied Gore on part of the safari.
- An account from F. George Heldt, an infantry man who also met Bostwick and penned Bostwick's recollections of the safari for an 1876 story in *Contributions of the Historical Society of Montana.*

Using these sources, painter Jack Roberts, in 1977, wrote *The Amazing Adventures of Lord Gore*, in an attempt to recount the Rocky Mountain safari in

This painting from Alfred Jacob Miller shows what Fort Laramie looked like in the 1830s, when it was still known as Fort William. *Library of Congress.*

a type of historical fiction in which the unknown details are invented by the author. Twenty years later, in 1997, another Gore biography was published, *Baronet in an Earth Lodge*, in which researcher Barry C. Johnson constructed a more scholarly work, writing only that which could be backed up by primary sources. Johnson, in his book, took a jab at Roberts for filling in the blanks with his own assumptions about Gore's life and surmising the details that were unknown to him.

Here's Johnson issuing a comical criticism of Roberts's work:

> *When it came to the hunt,* [Roberts] *was understandably frustrated by the dearth of reliable information: if he was to paint, he had to invent and (his own word) to "surmise." This can be accepted as legitimate artistic license, but Mr. Roberts has surrounded his paintings and drawings with about sixty large pages of text. Here, his frequent surmises take on an air of fact and are supplemented by entirely irrelevant diversions during which Gore and Bridger are quite lost to view.*[117]

Johnson's critique of Roberts is humorous because it's such an excellent example of history repeating itself. Nearly fifty years earlier, in 1952, a widely distributed story in *The Cattlemen Magazine* shared details of Gore's adventure that likely contained some embellishment of the story, although it's hard to tell, as no sources were cited. This was followed, in 1959, by the first article to be written about Gore that was a scholarly work—with sources cited—a *Montana Magazine* piece titled "A Celtic Nimrod in the Old West," by Clark C. Spence. In it, Spence, amid all his painstaking work to acknowledge the foundations of his research, took a subtle jab at *The Cattlemen* for not doing the same.

Here's Spence criticizing *The Cattlemen*'s work:

> *"At night," says one writer in a flight of fancy, "*[Gore's] *camp looked like the bridal suite at the Waldorf." Imported serving men in costly livery and powdered wigs, fine sterling silver mugs (Gore would drink from no other), chest after chest of select wines and liqueurs, gold-plated buffalo guns—all of these may or may not have existed. But if they did, documentation is lamentably lacking.*[118]

At the risk of enduring some future condemnation as a surmiser in a flight of fancy (while attempting to inoculate against it with documentation that is not lamentably lacking), I've pulled together a supercut of Gore's story, borrowing material from not only the scholars Johnson and Spence but also Roberts and some of the other less-reliable sources as well, despite the criticism they've received. Ultimately, Gore has become a household name in Colorado due to the legend he took on following his journey, and that legend grew as a result of all of his stories, whether they are completely true or not. Spence may have said it best when he wrote of Gore's safari, "It is historical fact, but it is the stuff from which historical novels are written." Colorado journalist Forbes Parkhill, in his 1951 compilation of stories titled *The Wildest of the West*, went one step further and began a piece about Gore by placing it in the framework through which every story is judged in modern times—its ability to translate to the silver screen.

"Hollywood never dreamed up anything with the *Arabian Nights* atmosphere of Gore's luxurious adventuring in our wide open spaces," Parkhill wrote, calling Gore the "Noblest Roamer of them All."[119]

A Hollywood logline of Gore's story might say that from 1854 to 1857, he traveled from St. Louis into the modern-day locations of Kansas, Nebraska, Colorado, Utah, Wyoming, Montana, South Dakota, North Dakota and down the Missouri River back to St. Louis again, and along the way, he was believed to have killed several thousand animals, built some of the

West's first wagon roads, discovered gold on three separate occasions, been murdered by Native tribes on two separate occasions, feuded with fur traders and U.S. government officials, burned most of his possessions in what has been called the most famous bonfire in the history of the West and spent a winter living among the Hidatsa tribe in an earth lodge made of grass and clay.

The long version of the story begins on May 24, 1854, when Gore was issued a passport by Colonel Alfred Cumming, the superintendent of Indian Affairs from the United States Central Division in St. Louis. With his permission to venture into Native territory granted, Gore and his massive crew headed toward Westport in the modern-day Kansas City area, where they set up camp in the area now occupied by Kansas City's Mission Hills Country Club. Bradley's story described Gore as having with him a wagon entirely loaded with arms, "of which he had some seventy-five rifles with a large number, twelve or fifteen, shotguns, and two wagons with Sir George's fishing tackle."

Bradley continued:

> *Sir George was abundantly supplied with everything necessary to his convenience and comfort. He had a large linen tent, about ten by eighteen feet, hung throughout with striped lining, a brass bedstead that unscrewed and packed in a small space, a portable iron table and iron washstand, and three milk cows. He carried with him also a splendid telescope with about a six-inch lens, supported upon a tripod, an instrument of great power. He was supplied with a large number of guns, single and double-barrel, of the best workmanship, all muzzle-loaders except one Sharp's rifle. He also had a large number of pistols of every description including revolvers.*[120]

A final detail from Bradley's story described a traveling wagon of peculiar design.

"It appeared like an ordinary open box-spring wagon, but by putting cranks on four points near the corners and turning all at once a top was lifted into view out of the bed, which converted it into a comfortable carriage or a bedroom," Bradley wrote.[121]

One of Gore's servants "was a skilled fly maker and was constantly gathering new material for flies," Bradley wrote. This is assumed to be Gore's close companion Alexander Mackenzie. A *New York Times* correspondent who encountered Gore's expedition while it was happening and wrote to the paper about it in 1857 said "one very accomplished person," likely

Mackenzie, was along on the expedition "simply to make artificial flies to entice foolish trout to the surface of babbling brooks."

That previously undiscovered report also said Gore had with him three tons of ammunition, which he brought from England, "besides all sorts and descriptions of guns, pistols, dogs, fishing tackle, and other things entirely too numerous to mention."[122]

When Gore left Westport in June 1854, an *Ohio State Journal* correspondent witnessed the party's departure, saying Gore had with him "between forty and fifty dogs, mostly grey-hounds and stag hounds, of the most beautiful breeds," along with "a large carriage, and probably a dozen large wagons to transport provisions," which required "five yoke of oxen to each wagon."[123]

But by the time Gore met up with Bostwick in 1855, he was down to only fourteen dogs, as Heldt noted in his retelling of Bostwick's story, meaning the Gore party must have lost quite a few dogs along the way. It's likely they were using the exotic British animals for trading currency, because for years in the Gore party's wake, stories surfaced of English hounds inhabiting areas the party had traveled. Captain Eugene F. Ware, in his 1911 book, *The Indian War of 1864*, recalled visiting Fort Kearney in Nebraska in the 1860s and encountering a large number of greyhounds running around the fort:

> *The origin of these greyhounds was as follows, which I give as it was told to me. Sometime back in the '50s, an English nobleman by the name of Lord George Gore came to this country for the purpose of hunting big game. As one person described it to me, Lord George Gore came with forty horses, forty servants, forty guns, forty dogs and forty of everything else. He stopped at Fort Kearney and hunted, and several litters of these greyhounds, and some of the original bunch, were left at the post, and became sort of public property, subject to the direction of the post commander.*[124]

In addition to those 14 greyhounds, Heldt's recording of Bostwick's story said Gore had 40 men, 112 horses, 12 yoke of cattle, 6 wagons and 21 carts,[125] while Bradley's recording of Bostwick's story said Gore had 41 men, 4 6-mule wagons, 2 3-yoke ox wagons and 21 red river carts, each drawn by 2 horses.[126] Marcy, the army captain who met Gore in 1857, said the party consisted of approximately 50 persons, a train of 30 wagons, numerous saddle horses and dogs and "guns of various descriptions and calibers, suited to the destruction of all kinds of game." In examining those weapons, Marcy said he observed "the names of Joe Manton, Purdy, Westley Richards, and other celebrated makers."[127]

Captain Randolph B. Marcy.
Wikimedia Commons.

A story about one weapon in particular was recently uncovered by Jim Bridger's biographer, Jerry Enzler. Enzler found several previously undiscovered details about Gore after scouring the journals of Robert Campbell, the famous St. Louis frontiersman turned businessman who helped Gore outfit his adventure. The weapon of Gore's, discovered by Enzler, was described by Bridger as the best gun he ever handled, a gun "so unique it required special instructions for loading," Enzler wrote. Gore later sold the rifle to the Blair family, of the famous Blair House in Washington, D.C., for $260, estimated to be the equivalent of nearly $10,000 today.[128]

It's not recorded where Gore contracted with the forty to fifty men he brought with him on his expedition, but Enzler's findings show Bridger was hired in St. Louis. Henry (with a *y*) Chatillon, nephew of the famous guide Henri (with an *i*) Chatillon, said his uncle Henri was contracted in St. Louis as well.[129] It has been previously assumed that, in addition to Bridger and Henri Chatillon, Gore hired the rest of his men in St. Louis after his bank drafts were paid out in March 1854. Those bank drafts have always been considered the first mention of Gore in the United States, but a *St. Louis Intelligencer* article I recently discovered from a month earlier says that when Gore arrived in St. Louis in late 1853, he already had with him a large retinue of hunters, so it's likely that many of Gore's forty men had been with him for longer than previously assumed, accompanying him on his winter 1853–54 expedition to the Texas/Mexico area.[130]

After the crew left St. Louis in May 1854, it appears that they traveled first to Westport and then on to Fort Kearney before they finally landed at Fort Laramie in Wyoming. They probably took the Oregon Trail as their route, as Heldt said they traveled along the north fork of the Platte River, where that famous trail was laid. Henri Chatillon was leading the expedition at that point, and he knew the Oregon Trail well, being the subject of Francis Parkman's 1849 book, *The Oregon Trail.* Chatillon and Parkman kept in touch for years following their expedition, and Chatillon mentioned Gore in his letters to Parkman, describing Gore as "disagreeable" and saying they parted ways after eleven months.[131]

Chatillon's nephew Henry said his uncle Henri was hired in St. Louis at the beginning of the expedition in April or May 1854, so that means he would have departed the group during the spring of 1855. At that point, it appears Bridger had already taken over as guide; the group's tour south from Fort Laramie into Colorado had already occurred in 1854, as evidenced by the carvings they left in the trees atop Gore Pass, where Bridger guided Gore. Bostwick also said that when he joined the group in 1855, he had heard that they spent much of 1854 in the "parks" of Colorado, probably referring to the areas of North Park and Middle Park, near the road they built, which is now known as Gore Pass.

The Gore party is said to have made its first discovery of gold at some point before reaching Colorado during the summer or fall of 1854, in a location fifty or seventy miles southwest of Fort Laramie in Wyoming. Henry Chatillon recounted the story in an 1897 letter to *The Denver Evening Post*, saying Louis Dapron, who was part of the Gore party, found something that looked like gold in a creek and brought it back to camp.

"They showed the gold to M. Gore," Chatillon wrote, "and as soon as he laid his eyes on it he said this is gold, but I did not come here to seek gold. I don't need it; I am on a pleasure hunt."

Roberts surmised that this discovery was probably made on Douglas Creek near Centennial, Wyoming, in the area which would become the future site of the New Rambler Mine. In 1869, about $8,000 worth of gold was taken from the area using ordinary gold panning methods.[132]

Chatillon said Gore broke camp immediately and departed the area, "because this gold find might cause all his men to leave."[133]

From there, the Gore party headed down to modern-day Colorado, but exactly what route they took is not known. Besides Bridger's recollection of guiding Gore over the pass, which he repeated years later when taking Edward L. Berthoud along that same route, the most we know of Gore's time in Colorado is what was printed in Chatillon's 1897 letter to *The Denver Evening Post*. Henry's uncle Henri and his brother, Joseph Chatillon (Henry's father), were with the expedition during the Colorado adventure, and Henry Chatillon also knew another man, Louis Dapron, who he said was on that part of the expedition. Drawing from Henry Chatillon's letter and, perhaps, some of his own reporting, Parkhill said Gore was camped out in Colorado's Middle Park when he learned that elk were numerous on the far side of a nearby mountain range.

Jim Bridger. *Wikimedia Commons.*

"Legend has it that he employed a tribe of 800 Indians to cut a road through the timber so his wagon train could cross the range and then remained only four days on the far side," Parkhill wrote.[134]

In *Baronet in an Earth Lodge*, Johnson wrote he was doubtful of the legend that Gore hired a tribe of Native workers to cut his road, calling it "preposterous" and saying, "the idea of hiring a tribe of Indians for such work is extremely fantastic and may be taken as pure invention." Johnson was also able to obtain a letter from Parkhill, in which Parkhill said he believed the story of Natives cutting Gore Pass came from Bridger.[135]

Johnson may have believed the story to be fiction because Bridger was known to exaggerate, but Bridger's style of telling tall tales was done for humorous effect, usually with a punchline at the end that revealed the story to be "preposterous," in Johnson's words. And many times, there was a kernel of truth on which Bridger's stories were founded, so those stories often were not, to again use Johnson's words, "pure invention."

A good example of this comes from famous Civil War General William T. Sherman, who recounted a conversation between Bridger and a comrade who had heard about trees that had turned to stone.

"Them's called petrifications," Bridger said, according to Sherman. "Come with me to the Yellowstone next summer and I will show you petrified trees a-growing with petrified birds singing petrified songs."

Sherman then, reflecting on the humorous tale, described how there were indeed petrified trees in Yellowstone.

"So Jim Bridger's story was not all a lie, only partly so," Sherman said.[136]

Many of Bridger's descriptions of Yellowstone and the West were regarded with skepticism at first, only to be found to be accurate in the end. Bridger said he knew of a spot where trout could swim across the Continental Divide, and this has been proven true in the area known as North Two Ocean Creek. Bridger also said he knew of a place where he could catch a trout in cold water and have it cooked by the time he reeled it in, and indeed, in Yellowstone National Park, there are places where trout streams exist next to thermal features with scalding hot water. People also did not believe Bridger when he said he knew of a high mountain lake that was sixty miles long, a place where geysers spout up to seventy feet high at regular intervals and an acid spring that gushes out in a river torrent. These turned out to be the Yellowstone Lake, the Yellowstone Geyser Basins and Mammoth Hot Springs, all real places.[137]

With all this in mind, I'm not as quick to dismiss Bridger's account of Gore hiring eight hundred Native road builders as pure invention. Perhaps it's an exaggeration, and Gore hired only a fraction of that amount of people to cut those roads, but a simple fact remains that Johnson is too quick to discount: the fact that the road exists! A winding, twenty-five-mile-long mountain road was indeed carved out of the Colorado wilderness by someone. Cutting a road of that size in that area would have been a difficult feat for Gore's men to accomplish in the limited amount of time they spent there, and Native tribes were known to frequent that path. The Northern Ute tribe occupied the elk and deer hunting grounds on the west side of the pass, known as Old Park, and the Southern Arapahoe tribe seasonally occupied the buffalo hunting grounds on the east side, known as Middle Park.

"The Gore Range separated these two excellent hunting grounds," Roberts wrote. "In Lord Gore's day, the only possible vehicular route across that range was by way of the natural pass that bears his name today. It was an Indian trail long before the arrival of that aristocratic hunter, and since the Utes and the Arapahos were forever enemies, it could appropriately be called a warpath. Jim Bridger had long known of that warpath across those mountains."[138]

Bridger and Gore are assumed to have first arrived in Middle Park on the east side of the pass. Once there, if they indeed encountered the Southern Arapahoe—who numbered about 1,500 by 1850—they could have hired a large number of the tribe's members to widen their warpath into a wagon road. Bridger, who was able to speak many Native languages, would have been able to translate and broker this deal. No account of the expedition mentions Gore's men cutting any roads over mountain passes, so Bridger's recollections are all that can be depended on when determining how that road got there. If Bridger said it was cut by 800 Natives, the stipulation that he was known to tell tall tales along with his true tales isn't reason enough, in my view, to discount the story as pure fiction.

Gore no doubt heard his own fair share of tall tales from Bridger, which may have been why he was said to have enjoyed reading to Bridger the stories of Baron Munchhausen. Munchhausen was an eighteenth-century Russian

An 1872 painting of Baron Munchausen, by August von Wille. *Wikimedia Commons.*

officer who became famous for telling outrageous tales about his military adventures, inspiring German writer Rudolf Erich Raspe to create a fictional version of him (Baron Munchausen) who, in Raspe's stories, relayed first-person accounts of impossible feats, like riding cannonballs and traveling to the moon.

Gore Creek. *Scott Cramer.*

Gore Creek. *Scott Cramer.*

Above: Gore Creek, with Vail Ski Resort in the background. *Scott Cramer.*

Left: A stand-up paddleboarder and a kayaker on Gore Creek. *Scott Cramer.*

A tent in the Gore Range. *Scott Cramer.*

An angler on Gore Lake. *Scott Cramer.*

A mountain goat in the Gore Range. *Scott Cramer.*

Ski touring in the Gore Range. *Scott Cramer.*

A skier with the Gore Range in the background. *Scott Cramer.*

The town of Vail in the Gore Creek Valley. *Scott Cramer.*

Gore Canyon and the Union Pacific Railroad line. *Scott Cramer.*

Gore Creek Drive in Vail Village. *Scott Cramer.*

The Gore Lake Trail. *Scott Cramer.*

Gore Pass. *Scott Cramer.*

A water hazard near Gore Creek at the Vail Golf Club, with the Gore Range in the background. *Scott Cramer.*

Gore Lake. *Scott Cramer.*

The ski slopes of Vail, with the Gore Range in the background. *Scott Cramer.*

The Gore Range. *Scott Cramer.*

The Gore Range. *Scott Cramer.*

The Gore Range. *Scott Cramer.*

The Gore Range. *Scott Cramer.*

The Gore Range. *Scott Cramer.*

The Gore Range. *Scott Cramer.*

The Gore Range. *Scott Cramer.*

High above Gore Canyon. *Scott Cramer.*

The Gore Range. *Scott Cramer.*

The Gore Range. *Scott Cramer.*

The Gore Range. *Scott Cramer.*

The Gore Range. *Scott Cramer.*

The Gore Range. *Scott Cramer.*

The Gore Range. *Scott Cramer.*

The Gore Range. *Scott Cramer.*

Army Captain Randolph B. Marcy knew Bridger well and also met Gore in 1857; he said both Gore and Bridger told him about their expedition. Marcy described several scenes in which Gore would read books to Bridger in the evenings, saying Bridger called Baron Munchhausen "a durn'd liar," but added that he "acknowledged that some of his own experience among the Blackfeet would be equally marvelous, 'ef writ down in a book.'"[139]

One of Bridger's tall tales about the Blackfeet, likely based on some truth but ending in a comical twist, involves him being chased by the tribe's warriors for miles across the rugged lands of the West. As Bridger reached the point of the story where a Blackfeet warrior was closing in on him and he found himself trapped at the end of a box canyon, he was known to pause and wait for his listeners to ask what happened. Bridger would then deadpan the response: "He killed me." This story was dramatized in the television program *The Tall Tales of Jim Bridger*, which ran for one season on the INSP network in 2024.

Unlike INSP, Gore continued to renew Bridger, season after season, from 1854 to 1857. Retaining Bridger was a testament to Gore's ability to recognize the top talent of his day, as Bridger was indeed the most sought-after guide and the most respected mountain man in the West during the 1850s. He was noted for predicting when bad weather was on its way, when one route favored another and when skirmishes, battles and even all-out wars were on the horizon. The fact that Gore thrived for three years in a wilderness that was often hostile to settlers should be largely attributed to Bridger and his ability to stay out of trouble. But Gore's intuition in trusting Bridger—perhaps influenced by the death of his friend some fifteen years earlier on the Falls of Doonass—is proven to have been keen in the American West.

Bridger and Gore may have seemed an odd couple, but they were reported to have gotten along well. An 1872 *Chicago Tribune* profile of Bridger describes his relationship with Gore as one in which cultural differences were openly mocked amid an overarching atmosphere of mutual respect for one another's hunting skills, making the two sound a bit like the yet-to-be-invented J.R.R. Tolkien characters Gimli and Legolas:

> *Often* [Bridger] *would, when excited by Sir George's fine sportsmanship, break out with, "I declar* [sic], *Mr. Gore, what a pity it is you are an Englishman, for you are a real good shot." Gore, on such occasions, would only laugh at him, and say that he hoped, by being good, some day to merit the honor of becoming a plain citizen; whereupon Bridger would*

> *encourage him, and innocently inquire, "Won't they allow you to resign your* Sir *commission?"*[140]

Bridger and Gore, Parkhill wrote, stayed only on the far side of Gore Pass for four days after constructing their legendary wagon road across the northern part of what would later be known as the Gore Range. Parkhill quoted Henry Chatillon's 1897 letter to *The Denver Evening Post*, which said that the party continued through Middle Park, crossing the Continental Divide and camping on all four sides of Pikes Peak, suggesting that years later, "the discovery of log bridges over mountain streams where no wheeled vehicles had been known to have penetrated" was likely from the Gore party in 1854.[141]

"If this be true," Parkhill wrote, "and Gore built his own roads for his wagon train through some of the most rugged mountain terrain in the United States, he performed a feat unequaled in the history of Western exploration."

But as Johnson notes of Gore's foray into Colorado, "No part of his excursion is so much of a blank as its first stage."[142] And the newspaper stories that did attempt to piece together the Colorado leg of Gore's journey are slight on sources. One story from *The Steamboat Pilot*, written in 1964, said that in addition to Middle Park, Gore also hunted in South Park (where the town of Fairplay is located today), which would have been precisely en route to the Pike's Peak area. The story, which bears no byline and cites no sources, says Gore traveled through Summit County to get to Fairplay. The story appears to be based on the same legend that Parkhill cited—those reports of roads and bridges being found where no wheeled vehicles had been before.

"Gore, with a retinue of his men, followed up the Blue (a river in Summit County, Colorado), passing the present site of Breckenridge and over Hoosier pass," the *Pilot* reported. "They cut roads thru timber and made roads around steep hillsides. They made preparations for fording streams, carrying with them all the tools and other appurtenances necessary to overcome all obstacles incident to mountain travel in those days of savage life."[143]

If Gore was taking cues from his fellow British traveler Charles William Wentworth Fitzwilliam, then it's possible his party took the Hoosier Pass route in an effort to reach Bent's New Fort on the Santa Fe Trail southwest of Pike's Peak. That was one of the last stops Fitzwilliam made before returning to St. Louis, and Jim Bridger would have been a familiar face there as well.[144] From Bent's New Fort, in the flatlands of Colorado's Front Range—with winter approaching—it would have been a much easier journey due north

Gore Pass. *Scott Cramer.*

to Fort Laramie in Wyoming, where we know the party spent the winter of 1854–55. That route might have taken Trapper's Trail, a road well known to Bridger and his business partner, Louis Vasquez, who was also on the Gore expedition. Trapper's Trail followed roughly what is now Interstate 25, through the location of the former Fort Vasquez, which Vasquez founded and later sold.

The recollections of General Bela M. Hughes, published in *The Denver News* in 1865 and *The Steamboat Pilot* in 1902, is another source that suggests this route is possible. When Hughes reached what he called "the Bear river valley," which is the modern-day Yampa River Valley south of Steamboat Springs, he said he found one of Gore's camps, saying Gore came "from Ft. Laramie through Ft. Bridger."[145] This would mean the party traveled west from Fort Laramie all the way to Southwest Wyoming along the Green River Valley, where Fort Bridger was located, before heading back east into Ute territory in modern-day Colorado on the west side of Gore Pass. From there, they would have continued heading east, building Gore Pass from west to east, eventually reaching the Blue River near modern-day Kremmling and continuing south along the Blue River, as the *Pilot* reported in its 1964 story.[146]

Scott Cramer.

In his 1897 letter to the *Denver Evening Post*, Henry Chatillon said his father, Joseph Chatillon, joined the Gore party at Fort Bridger as well. Other writers—who weren't aware of Hughes's letter—assumed Chatillon meant Fort Laramie, but with two different sources suggesting the Fort Bridger route was taken, perhaps it deserves more consideration. A piece of physical evidence that suggests the party took the Fort Bridger route is an axletree that Hughes found south of Fort Bridger in Utah Territory on the Uinta River, near the modern-day Colorado-Wyoming border. This find from Hughes was reported in *The Denver News* in 1865, and Hughes was so certain the axletree was Gore's that he told the paper he intended to take it to St. Louis "for the purpose of having a cane made from it to present to the former owner of the timber."[147]

Bridger had good relations with the Utes and had been married to a Ute woman a few years earlier, so it's plausible that he may have brokered a deal with that tribe to cut Gore Pass from west to east. In the early 1870s, when Major John Westley Powell used Gore Pass to travel through Colorado on his surveys of the West, he brought with him photographer John K. Hillers, who took an interest in the Ute people. Hillers took two photographs of Ute men with dogs, and the dogs he photographed do not at all resemble those commonly associated with the Native tribes of the area—the long-haired, wolf-like animals known as the American Indian dog. The dogs Hiller photographed looked much more like the short-haired English staghounds Gore was reported to have had with him,[148] which could have been good currency for Gore in his attempts to bargain with local tribes. Gore was reported to have left Westport with forty to fifty dogs; when he reached Fort Laramie, he was down to just fourteen, and when he finally ended his expedition years later, Gore was reported to have had only one dog with him, an American Indian dog.[149]

Regardless of the route the Gore party took, we know that when they reached Fort Laramie in the late fall or early winter of 1854, Bridger found a letter from Campbell waiting for him, dated September 23. It informed him that his youngest son, four-year-old John Bridger, had died of bilious dysentery during the summer of 1854. Bridger then left Vasquez in charge as he departed Fort Laramie to check on his family.[150]

Fort Laramie is where Bostwick's account of the Gore expedition picks up. Bostwick joined Gore's group during the spring of 1855, and because he told his story to two different people who took down and published the details he shared, we have much more information about the Gore expedition after its Colorado leg ended.

U.S. Army infantryman F. George Heldt, a writer who published Bostwick's memories of the Gore expedition in 1876, said the party enjoyed "the wild delights of the chase" at Fort Laramie during the winter of 1854–55.

"The isolation of this fort at that early time excelled that of any other fort in the West, and the wild hunters, trappers, traders, and adventurers who made that their headquarters and occasional rendezvous, were a motley group of characters worthy a winter's experience, and Sir George made them an interesting study," Heldt wrote. "Here, too, he made the acquaintance of some of the Indian tribes upon whose hunting grounds he was about to intrude; and what with the traders, the hunters, the soldiers, and the Indians, the water sped pleasantly away."[151]

While at Fort Laramie, Bostwick witnessed an interaction involving Gore and trader Joseph Bissonet (sometimes spelled Bissonette) that foreshadowed a side of Gore that would be seen again later. Bradley recounted it in his journal:

> *At Fort Laramie, Sir George had an agreement with Bissonette to supply his party with cattle for beef at forty dollars a head. Sir George paid this price so promptly and readily that it occurred to Bissonette to try to practice*

> *a little extortion, Sir George was wealthy and would hardly complain if he had to pay a little more for his beef, and so he raised the price to sixty dollars a head, but the result was Sir George promptly ceased to deal with him and would not buy another head at any price.*[152]

The payment to Bissonet was made by Robert Campbell back in St. Louis. In a letter from April 1855, Campbell told Gore that he paid Bissonet $2,000 and requested that Gore "take such steps as will place me in funds at an early day." Campbell also let Gore know that Bridger had not yet made it

Opposite and above: Ute men with their dogs, circa 1871. *John K. Hillers, Library of Congress.*

to St. Louis from Westport to secure more supplies for the party at that point, because Bridger had a "very severe attack of pneumonia and had to stop at Sibley (along the Missouri River)."[153]

The next time Gore heard from Campbell, it was more than a month later in a letter dated May 24, 1855. Campbell had not heard back from Gore following his last letter, and he appeared to be getting nervous that his funds had not yet been received from England:

> *I have received for you a gun from England upon which I have paid duty and freight, the sum of $114.70. I will endeavor to have it forwarded to you soon. I have not yet received any advice from any agent of your authorizing me to draw upon them on your account. I beg that you will take such steps as will place me in funds at as early a day as possible as it is inconvenient to be out of my funds so long. I feel quite well assured that the delay is occasioned by some mistake of your instructions to your agent. James Bridger has been here....He said you spoke of sending an order for carts and articles to be taken up for your use, but no letter has been received from you.*[154]

The Gore party remained at Fort Laramie, with Bridger's business partner Louis Vasquez in charge, for the entire summer of 1855. The party's failure to depart the fort during the summer was likely due to Bridger's delay in getting to St. Louis and Gore's delay in getting Campbell

Above: A view of the interior of Fort Laramie in the 1830s, from painter Alfred Jacob Miller. *Library of Congress.*

Opposite: Louis Vasquez. *Wikimedia Commons.*

his funds. While at Fort Laramie, Vasquez found himself mixed up in the early stages of the Sioux Wars, and he delivered a message that helped ignite General William S. Harney's brutal campaign against the Brule Lakota on September 3, 1855.

Both Vasquez and Gore are mentioned in one of the artifacts of that battle, the journal of Captain John Blair Smith Todd, which was published by the Nebraska State Historical Society in 1962. That publication contains a foreword by historian Ray H. Mattison, which explains the conflict:

The Harney Expedition in 1855 was the first of a number of campaigns conducted by the Army against the Sioux Indians which were not to end until Wounded Knee in 1890. During the first four decades of the 19th century, the relations between the whites and the Plains Sioux had been comparatively peaceful. However, by the middle of the century these had undergone a marked change.

The Sioux had welcomed the traders who built trading houses in their domain which supplied them with the much-desired white man's goods. Nor did they resent deeply the occasional bands of white trappers who invaded their domain and killed a few buffalo and other game for their own needs. The caravans of Oregon- and California-bound emigrants were a different breed. These white men coming in ever-increasing numbers as each year passed, brought their families, killed large amounts of game, established military posts, built permanent homes, and spread the dreaded cholera among them. For the first time, the Plains Sioux felt their security threatened.

In an effort to placate the red man and to settle the Indian question permanently, the Government made a treaty at Horse Creek near Fort Laramie in 1851 with several of the Plains tribes. By this treaty the Government defined the boundaries of a number of the Indian nations and guaranteed these lands against white aggression. The Indians in return recognized the right of the Government to establish roads and military posts in their respective territories and agreed not to commit depredations against travelers passing along the overland routes. For this concession the United States agreed to pay the Indians the sum of $50,000 each year in annuities for a term of fifty years.

Then in 1853 several Indians were killed as the result of a ferry boat incident at Fort Laramie. Although a number of the Indians were eager for retaliation, there was little disposition for a general war.

In August 1854 three Sioux tribes, the Brule, Oglala, and Miniconjou, were encamped on the Platte River about 8 miles east of Fort Laramie waiting for their annuities. A Mormon wagon train, destined for Salt Lake City, passed through the vicinity and a Miniconjou killed a cow seemingly deserted by the wagon train. Killing the cow violated the treaty and the owner of the cow reported the incident to the Commanding Officer at Fort Laramie as well as to the Chief of the Brule. After discussing the matter with an Oglala Chief, Man Afraid of His Horses, who was sent to him as an ambassador, the Commanding Officer sent Lieutenant John L. Grattan and a detachment of 29 men to bring in the offending Indian. In attempting to execute his order, the brash young lieutenant and his entire command were wiped out by the Indians.

When news of Grattan's fate reached the United States, the Army at once took steps to retaliate against the Indians.[155]

The Nebraska State Historical Society's publication then reprinted (as it originally appeared) the journal kept by Todd, who, in September 1855, encountered Vasquez as hostilities were about to commence between the six hundred troops with whom Todd was marching, led by Harney, and the Brule Lakota, led by Chief Little Thunder.

Sunday, 2 September: To day after marching six miles reached the crossing of the South Platte. The river is about one mile wide and is now very shallow. After crossing, continued the march to the North Platte & camped at the gorge of Ash Hollow. This noted point is a deep ravine connecting the high table lands between the two rivers and the valley of the North Platte. As we descended the hollow we could distinctly see the camp of a band of Brules. These people sent word to Genl Harney that if he wanted peace he could have it, or if he wanted war that he could have that. The chief also sent word that he would come in and see him. The bearer of this message was Mr. Vasquez who has for some time been attached to Sir Geo Gore's hunting party as chief guide. He is an old mountain man & Trader.[156]

Harney did not choose peace. His unit killed eighty-six Lakota in what was, at first, regarded as the Battle of Ash Hollow or the Battle of the Blue Water but is now better known as the Harney Massacre due to the number

Left: Captain John Blair Smith Todd. *Wikimedia Commons.*

Right: General William S. Harney. *Wikimedia Commons.*

of women and children killed. Gouverneur Kemble Warren, a mapmaker with the army, had been attached to Harney's unit and was horrified by what he saw. He wrote in his journal that during the battle, he saw children killed while in their mother's arms and women crying for their dead babies. When trying to help the wounded, he discovered "a little boy shot through the calves of his legs and through his hams….He had enough strength to hold me round the neck."[157]

When the slaughter was finished, a neighboring tribe of Oglala people came upon the site of the massacre, and among them was a ten-year-old boy named Curly who would go on to be known as Crazy Horse. He never forgot the scene and was said to have reminisced on it while planning the Battle of Little Bighorn, in which the famous Civil War Lieutenant George Armstrong Custer and his Seventh Cavalry Regiment were killed nearly twenty years later.[158]

Even though Gore and Vasquez were near the Harney Massacre, they managed to stay out of it, despite rumors to the contrary at the time. In its reporting on the Harney Massacre, *The St. Louis Republican*, during the fall of 1855, wrote that there "was a report that the Indians had attacked and killed the party of Sir George Gore," but that the rumor "was not believed at Fort Laramie."[159]

By the time that report hit newspapers, Gore had already settled up with Campbell, reunited with Bridger, resupplied his retinue and departed Fort Laramie. The party traveled along the west side of the Pumpkin Buttes in Northeast Wyoming, then down Powder River and up the Yellowstone River, with Gore "making frequent diversions to enjoy the delights of the chase," Heldt wrote, until reaching the Tongue River in Montana, "where he tarried a long time."[160]

Gore settled into a routine of sleeping until 10:00 or 11:00 a.m., having a bath, enjoying breakfast and a toddy and then setting out on the day's hunt. There are conflicting accounts of how Gore preferred to hunt, with Marcy (using both Bridger and Gore as his sources) writing that Gore "set out generally alone for the day's hunt,"[161] and Bradley, with Bostwick as his source, saying Gore "rarely, if ever, went unattended, his party usually comprising seven men."[162]

The discrepancy might come from Gore's description of his routine to Marcy, as Gore probably considered his daily departure with six attendants to be him hunting "alone," since no other hunters were there shooting animals with him. To Gore, who was accustomed to hunting the crowded highlands of Scotland alongside scores of other deer stalkers, he was indeed hunting by himself, because like his horses and dogs, his attendants were merely along for the purposes of servicing his own personal hunt. They themselves were not shooting animals.

Those attendants were responsible for keeping the weapons loaded, as Gore "never loaded his own gun, but after firing passed it to an attendant, who gave him another ready charged," Bradley wrote.[163] In that way, Gore could kill animals using the technique that made him famous on the moors when he killed six deer with six shots.

Gore would continue into the night—it wasn't unusual for him to remain out until 10:00 p.m., Marcy wrote—and "he seldom returned to camp without augmenting the catalogue of his exploits."[164]

With that detail, I think it's important to point out that Marcy did take down some of Gore's numbers from that catalogue, writing in his book *Thirty Years of Army Life on the Border* that Gore killed 40 grizzly bears and 2,500 buffalo. We can compare that to Indian Agent Alfred J. Vaughan, who, in an 1856 letter, stated that Gore said he had killed 105 bears, 1,600 elk and deer and 2,000 buffalo. Since Vaughan appeared to quote Gore directly and his figure is also reasonably close to what Marcy wrote, the

Montgomery C. Meigs. *Wikimedia Commons.*

2,000 to 2,500 figure is what has generally been accepted as the most accurate tally of Gore's bison slaughter.

But another account that was relayed to the secretary of the interior in 1856 says Gore killed six thousand buffalo. This count came from, of all people, Montgomery C. Meigs, a Washington, D.C.–based civil engineer who was working on an extension of the Capitol's post office building at the time. Meigs did not provide a source for his information, but the fact that he would know anything at all about Gore's hunt shows the waves it was making across the country. Other writers have been quick to dismiss Meigs's figures as exaggeration, but perhaps the engineer, amid all his time spent at the post office, had better information than we realize. Meigs attended West Point at the same time as Captain John Blair Smith Todd (who mentioned Vasquez and Gore in his journal from Ash Hollow in 1855), so it's plausible that they knew each other and were in contact. Meigs referenced the Harney Massacre at Ash Hollow in his letter about Gore's slaughter, saying "we punish an Indian for killing a settler's cow for food, how can such destruction of their game be permitted by their friends in the Government of the United States?"[165]

The reason I'm not as quick to dismiss Meigs's six thousand buffalo claim is because I discovered a detail that has been overlooked by the others who have studied Gore, a crucial bit of reporting from Marcy.

When Marcy published his book *Thirty Years of Army Life on the Border*, it was 1866, and at that time, he said he met Gore at the end of Gore's hunt in 1857. But what has been previously undiscovered is the fact that Marcy actually published an account of his time spent with Gore immediately after meeting him in 1857 in a piece for *The New York Herald*. Marcy's 1857 story for the *Herald* is not much different than what he later published in his 1866 book but for one notable exception—in the *Herald* story, printed just after he met Gore, Marcy wrote that Gore killed "122 grizzly bears, 2,500 buffaloes; besides numerous elk, black tailed deer and antelope—in all amounting to the enormous aggregate of 3,600 animals," importantly, "*during one season.*"[166] Compare that to his book, which was written nine years later, when his memory for the details might not have been as good, and we see Marcy never mentions that the death toll of 2,500 bison was amassed during a single season. The many writers who referenced that 2,500 figure in the years that followed looked only at Marcy's book, not his *Herald* story, and assumed it to have been Gore's cumulative total.

When you consider the "during one season" detail from Marcy's 1857 story, along with the fact that Gore had been hunting in the United States for longer than most have assumed, actually arriving in 1853 and hunting that entire winter season as well (in the region simply referred to as "Texas," which absolutely could have included bison habitat), suddenly, that six thousand figure doesn't seem so far-fetched.

One thing we can say for certain is that Gore killed a lot of bison during the fall of 1855, when he was enjoying his leisurely mornings and late nights along the Powder and Yellowstone Rivers in modern-day Wyoming. At night, Gore would invite Bridger into his tent for dinner and drinks, which is where we get the Baron Munchausen story. Marcy wrote that "after a few glasses of wine had been drunk, [Gore] was in the habit of reading from some book, and eliciting from Bridger his comments thereon." Marcy said Gore also read to Bridger stories from Shakespeare and Sir Walter Scott, and in a continuation of their friendly rivalry, Gore and Bridger took jabs at each other over which army performed better, the British against the French at Waterloo or the American against the British during the War of 1812.[167] Gore's relative Lieutenant Colonel William Gore is said to have invented some of the military tactics used at Waterloo while he was a commanding officer of the Bristol Volunteers during the Napoleonic Wars, and Gore was likely familiar with that bit of family lore and therefore especially partial to the English performance at Waterloo.[168] Marcy wrote that Gore asked Bridger if Waterloo was not "the most sanguinary battle he had ever heard of," to which Bridger responded that the British "must a fit better" at Waterloo than they had at the Battle of New Orleans in 1815.

When that season concluded, the party moved up the Yellowstone to the Tongue River in modern-day Montana under Bridger's guidance. Eight miles from the mouth of the Tongue River, Gore ordered a fort to be erected, which included stables, storehouses and living quarters. The party intended to spend the winter there, Bradley wrote, "but unfortunately, Bostwick set the woods on fire by accident, destroying all the grass in the vicinity so that it became necessary to seek new grazing grounds at the mouth of Tongue river."[169]

Some of the men stayed behind in the fort, but the animals needed to be moved to a new area at the mouth of the Tongue River, where there were more suitable grazing grounds. Gore ordered a new building to be constructed there, and he spent the winter of 1855–56 in it with his favorite horse, a Kentucky Thoroughbred he named Steel Trap.

"During the winter each man was required to gather one hundred and twenty-five pounds of cottonwood bark as forage for the animals, but Sir George fed his favorite horse upon cornmeal," Bradley wrote.[170]

Gore knew a good horse when he saw one. At one point during his expedition, Gore met Joseph Merrival, a fur trader who was married to a Sioux woman and served as a Sioux interpreter, and purchased from him a horse for $150. After riding the horse, Gore told Merrival, "I have tried the horse I bought from you and find him worth more than you ask. Here is one hundred dollars more, which makes the cost nearer his true value."[171]

The story, which came from Bostwick via Bradley, is consistent with what was a standard modus operandi for Gore, which was to buy the best animals he could whenever he could. Later in life, Gore would spend much of his time competing in dog shows and poultry exhibitions, where he often earned top honors. In an 1891 recollection of working for Gore some twenty-seven years earlier, an English writer who went by the handle "Old Turk" said Gore was known for having the best canines and poultry of the day, "due, in great measure to the fact that, if he saw or knew of anyone having a better dog or bird than he had, he would purchase it if at all possible, no matter what the price was."

Old Turk also recalled the name of one of Gore's favorite dogs, "Young Trap," which was the offspring of another of his prized dogs, "Old Trap." It's remarkable how well this story of Young Trap, Gore's prized dog in England, lines up with the story of Steel Trap, Gore's prized horse in the American West.

From Old Turk: "Sir George kept but one dog as a companion and house dog to sleep in the hall, and this was the celebrated fox terrier Young Trap."[172]

From Bostwick: "Sir George caused to be built for his own use a small log building, into which he also admitted his favorite horse, Steel Trap."[173]

While Gore wintered in that small log building with Steel Trap, Bridger again returned to Westport to be with his family, with plans to return in the spring. During the winter, one of Gore's men, known simply as "Uno," died of an unstated cause. His comrades proposed to bury him in his clothes due to a lack of lumber, "but Sir George caused the bed of one of his wagons to be taken to pieces and a coffin made from the material which he lined with cloth from his stores," Bradley wrote. "His kindness of heart is further shown by his writing to the relatives of the deceased offering to bring home the remains, if they desired."

The story is another from Bradley that paints Gore in a favorable light, and with Bostwick as his source, this should be expected. Bostwick was himself a beneficiary of Gore's "kindness of heart," as, upon his departure from the party, Bostwick asked to purchase a cart and some other supplies from Gore's steward, who "not only gave Bostwick all he asked for but added so many articles that he had not called for that Bostwick became alarmed and told the steward that he hadn't money to pay for so much," Bradley wrote. "The steward went to Sir George and received the orders: 'Let him have the goods and charge him twelve dollars,'" even though Bostwick had several hundred dollars' worth of wares in his possession.

The suspicion of that transaction creating a friendly bias toward Gore in Bostwick's recollections could explain why Bradley's recounting of Gore's interactions with the Native tribes in the area, via Bostwick, would later differ from those alleged during the winter 1856–57 by Indian Agent Alfred J. Vaughn and Major Alexander Culbertson.

While Gore was wintering during the 1855–56 season, members of the Piegan Blackfeet tribe were alleged to have stolen twenty-one of Gore's horses. They were pursued by eleven of Gore's men for some sixty miles without success, as "a heavy snowstorm completely obliterated the trail," Bradley wrote. Following this incident, the Kainai Nation, another tribe within the Blackfoot Confederacy, attempted to steal more of Gore's horses, "but the noise made by them in removing the pickets roused the men and Sir George's cook fired, wounding Major Culbertson's brother-in-law, Big Plumb, who was one of the marauding party, whereupon the Indians fled without securing any horses."[174]

That kicked off a controversy with Culbertson, which culminated the following season, after Gore and his men reunited with Bridger and departed their self-constructed fort in the spring of 1856. The party then traveled south along the Tongue River toward Rosebud Creek, looking for a large Crow camp which they had heard about and wanted to visit.

Bridger was still guiding the party at that point, which explains why relations were good between the Gore party and the area's Native tribes. Bridger was beloved by the Crows, a fact that would become especially apparent ten years later when the tribe refused to attack U.S. government troops at Fort C.F. Smith because Bridger was living there and the Crows "would not permit Bridger to be endangered," according to a U.S. Army lieutenant on site at the time.[175]

Near Rosebud Creek, the Gore party was reported to have found gold for the second time. It was the late 1870s before anything was written about the discovery, but it had apparently become a part of local lore decades earlier. In April 1878, the *Montana Record-Herald* published a story about a local party that was preparing to prospect the Wolf Mountains area, "where gold was discovered nineteen or twenty years ago by a party of which Sir George Gore, Bridger, Mitch Boyer, and a Frenchman named Frazier, formed a part."

The *Record-Herald* reported that a nugget was plucked from the surface of the ground by a member of the Gore party.

"It was afterwards exhibited by Sir George Gore in St. Louis," the *Record-Herald* continued. "The place where it was found was about ten miles from where Gen. Crook had his fight with the Sioux on the Rosebud, in 1876."

After locating the Crow camp near the Rosebud in the spring of 1856, the Gore party traded with the Crows for a fresh supply of horses and readied for another summer season in the Rocky Mountain wilderness, Gore's third year of sequestering himself away from outside civilization. The timeline is sketchy, but at some point over the course of the next year, Gore's Western adventure reached its climactic conclusion, in which his party allegedly found gold once again, got robbed by the Sioux, feuded with fur traders and the federal government, enjoyed a spectacular bonfire containing many of Gore's belongings and spent some of the winter in the primitive earth lodge of a Native tribe. Also, at this point in the expedition, Gore is alleged to have called a tributary of the Yellowstone River in eastern Montana "Glendale" because it reminded him of a similar place in Ireland. The Glendale name morphed, over the years, into Glendive, which is what the creek and nearby town are named today.

After finding the Crow camp in the spring of 1856 and trading for fresh horses, the Gore party is said to have ventured off into the Black Hills area of modern-day South Dakota. Legend has it that Gore's men made their third discovery of gold while in the Black Hills, and just like with the first discovery, Gore is remembered for shunning the finding. This account came in 1875 from Jeremiah Proteau and was reprinted in several newspapers; I'm opting to share the version from the *Carson Daily Appeal* of Carson City for the hilarious bit of skepticism expressed in its setup:

> *Jeremiah Proteau is an old trapper and old trappers are tremendous liars; but here's what Jerry says about gold in the Black Hills: I left the Fur Company at Laramie and engaged with Sir George Gore as hunter and teamster. James Bridger was employed as guide. We left Laramie early in the fall for the Yellowstone country, taking a route which led us past the Black Hills, on the southern and eastern base, and reached the mouth of the Yellowstone late in November. We then marched up the Yellowstone to Tongue River, where we built a fort and remained for the winter, hunting and trapping. The following April we started with ten carts and forty men, crossed the head of the Rosebud, and went to the Big Horn river, where we built flat boats and floated down the Big Horn to the Yellowstone, and down that river to its mouth, where we met Sir George, who had made the trip by land. From there we came down the Missouri to the mouth of the Little Missouri, and up that stream to its head, then struck across on to the Belle Fourche, and down to the Bear Butte, and spent some time on the Swift or Rapid creek and Box Elder, in the Black Hills. One Sunday I went out to the falls of Swift creek with Lamourie. The falls were quite high and emptied into a broad basin. As we were standing by the falls I noticed some yellow looking stuff in the water, and I said to Lamourie—"By George! There's gold!" I took off my shirt and scooped up three double hands full of the yellow stuff and put it in my shirt. I said gold! He then looked at it a little while, when he said: "Oh no, Jerry, that's not gold, that's mica." I was not very well posted about gold and thought Sir George was. He took it and put it into two black bottles and placed them in his chest. The next day we marched out of the Black Hills, and two or three days after Bridger told me that Sir George told him it was gold. Sir George also told Lamourie that if he would prospect at the head of Swift creek he would find rich gold there. We left the Black Hills on account of the Indians, and when we got back to the Little Missouri we were attacked by about five hundred Indians who ran off all our horses.*[176]

The Daily Appeal's skepticism is important to note because when Proteau went public with this story in 1875, the so-called Black Hills gold rush was just beginning following the discovery of gold by the Custer Expedition of 1874. Gold-hungry prospectors were eager to hear corroborating stories of gold discoveries in the Black Hills, so the timing of Proteau's tale is suspicious, as it provided one more reason to violate the 1868 Treaty of Fort Laramie and support the removal of the Sioux Nation from the Black Hills.

The Chicago Tribune, in 1875, quoted one prospector as saying, "I know a feller who's been in them Hills…es fur back es '54, with Sir George Gore." The *Tribune* went on to express its displeasure with the campaign against the Sioux, writing "The question as to the ability of the military to accomplish the distasteful task assigned them is an open one in the minds of many," an eerie preview of the Battle of Little Bighorn.[177]

The Weekly Times-Democrat, in New Orleans, was also suspicious of Proteau's tale, writing:

> *Jeremiah Proteau, a citizen of the Yankton, an old trader, and one of the oldest inhabitants of what now forms Dakota territory, relates that while on a hunting expedition, in company with Sir George Gore in 1854, he scooped up "three double handfuls of the yellow stuff" at the foot of the falls of Swift Creek in the Black Hills. It is a very serious circumstance that of all the gold reported as discovered in that region none has reached the borders of civilization. The gold hunters who have visited the Hills have invariably returned in a dilapidated and starving condition. If the country were not "forbidden fruit" the probability is there would be very little, if any, excitement about it. When the Government shall have extinguished the Indian title, which it is now engaged in doing, we may get at the truth of these stories.*[178]

The discovery of gold by Custer's team in 1874 is, today, viewed as problematic, because if Custer was really there to set up a military post in the Black Hills area, as originally stated, then there would have been no reason for geologists to accompany him on the expedition. It's generally accepted today that the geologists joined Custer in the Black Hills because there had long been rumors of gold there, but where exactly those rumors sprang from is not fully known. Parkhill absolved Gore of any responsibility and in fact credited him with the opposite, writing, "Had [Gore] been less a sportsman he might have changed the history of the United States, for his discovery of gold easily could have led to the settlement of the West years earlier."[179]

The information that prompted the U.S. government to send geologists to the Black Hills on the Custer Expedition in 1874 is unknown, but what is known for certain is those geologists were indeed along on that expedition, and upon discovering gold and going public with the discovery, the area was flooded with prospectors violating the 1868 treaty.

The violations of the 1868 treaty stoked the coals of war, which had been smoldering since the Harney Massacre, and Custer ended up paying for it

Lieutenant Colonel George Armstrong Custer's wagon train passes through Castle Creek Valley in the Black Hills of South Dakota in 1874. *W.H. Illingworth, Library of Congress.*

with his life in 1876 at the Battle of Little Bighorn. One of the men from the Gore expedition, Mitch Boyer, was killed at Little Bighorn as well. Custer was portrayed as a martyr, and the nation, in mourning his death during the celebration of the centennial in July 1876, developed an appetite for revenge, resulting in the removal of the Lakota from the area. By the end of 1876, the U.S. military occupied the Black Hills.

After their expedition into the Black Hills in 1856, the Gore party headed north to Fort Union, a trading post of the American Fur Company that was located at the confluence of the Yellowstone and Missouri Rivers in what is now Northwest North Dakota. Heldt wrote that the party sent a good portion of its supplies to Fort Union by land, while others in the party, Gore included, constructed flat boats and floated the Yellowstone River to reach Fort Union. Once there, Gore's trouble with the U.S. government began. Gore realized, upon arrival, that Fort Union was being managed by Major Alexander Culbertson, the brother-in-law of Big Plumb of the Kainai Nation, whom Gore's cook shot during the attempted horse theft incident some months earlier.

"Not only did [Culbertson] resent the presence of the hunting party on 'his' territory, but he must have known that it was their rifle fire which had wounded his brother-in-law," Johnson wrote.[180]

Major Culbertson was joined at Fort Union by Colonel Alfred J. Vaughn, who, in July 1856, wrote a letter to Alfred Cumming, the superintendent of Indian Affairs who kicked off the Gore expedition by granting him his passport to travel through Indian Country in 1854. Vaughn's letter to Cumming said Gore had violated the passport, using his forty-three employees to build a fort in Crow country and, from that fort, trading "all kinds of Ind Goods Powder & Ball" with the Crows.

Vaughn said tribes in the area had been "loud in their complaints at men passing through their country killing and driving off their game," which is, along with another letter that would come from Vaughn a few months later, the origin of Gore's reputation for not having good relations with Native tribes while on his hunt.[181] But Bostwick, in his recollections of being on the hunt, said Gore "had very little difficulties with the Indians, never an engagement." In Bradley's retelling of Gore's story, using Bostwick as his source, Bradley had evidently read Vaughn's letter alleging that tribes had complained about Gore, as he specifically sought to discredit that charge by writing, "Bostwick says he never heard that the Indians complained of Sir George's destruction of game."[182] It should be remembered, however, that Bostwick had a favorable view of Gore after receiving his twelve-dollar bargain on several hundred dollars' worth of Gore goods.

Vaughn's letter is also where we get the claim that Gore killed (verbatim from the letter) "105 bears and some 2,000 buffalo, elk & deer 1,600 he states was more than they had any use for having killed it purely for sport."[183]

If he wasn't killing for the meat, Gore was probably killing for trophies, the collection of which must have been absolutely massive by the time he reached Fort Union in 1856. To get those trophies and his other belongings back to St. Louis, Gore hatched a plan to have two large boats constructed and sent down the Missouri River. He offered some of his remaining supplies to the officers stationed at Fort Union, who seemed happy to have them. Gouverneur Kemble Warren, the U.S. Army mapmaker who was horrified by what he witnessed at the Harney Massacre a year earlier, noted that he purchased two wagons, six mules and twelve horses from Gore.

Warren also sought Gore's help in crossing the Missouri River, and in his journal, he unwittingly refuted the *St. Louis Intelligencer*'s mean-spirited suggestion that the $400 Gore spent to ship his ferry boat "would not be valued at more than four hundred cents" to him in the West.

"Through the kindness of Sir Geo. Gore, who gave us use of his ferry boat and men to manage it…[we] crossed the river just above the mouth of the Yellowstone without any trouble whatever," Warren's assistant wrote in his journal.[184]

The American Fur Company agreed to take Gore's remaining supplies "at some stipulated price," Bostwick recalled, but when the construction of the boats that would float his supplies back to St. Louis was finished, "there was a misunderstanding as to the terms of the bargain."[185]

This is where we're reintroduced to the side of Gore seen back at Fort Laramie when he refused to do business with the cattle trader Joseph Bissonet after suspecting extortion. The misunderstanding over the terms of the American Fur Company's deal to take his remaining supplies and construct boats for him made Gore "mercurial, wrathful, effervescent, and reckless, and heedless of the consequences," Heldt wrote, based on the recollection of Bostwick, who was likely an eyewitness to the affair.

"[Gore] would not stand for the terms prescribed," Heldt continued. "He accordingly burned his wagons, and all the Indian goods and supplies not needed, in front of the fort, guarding the flames from the plunder of whites and Indians."[186]

The conflagration, described in *Baronet in an Earth Lodge*, was "probably the most famous bonfire in the history of the West."[187] It is a dramatic conclusion that has tantalized, for a century and a half, every writer who has researched Gore. Roberts, amid the criticism of his frequent "surmises," spends most of his book building up to the bonfire after teasing it in his foreword, using it as a justification for those surmises.

"An objective historian could well ask, 'How can you prove Lord Gore got drunk after he set fire to his wagons?'" Roberts wrote in his foreword. "Well, I can't prove it. I can only reply that it is very difficult for me to imagine that he would stay sober on such an occasion."[188]

Roberts, 164 pages later, describes Gore as having a "rip-roaring, hell-raising blast in good ol' mountain man style…where the blazes of his sacrificial fire had scorched the very gates of Fort Union."[189]

After turning their backs on the scorched gates of Fort Union, the Gore party traveled east along the Missouri River to Fort Berthold. Roberts surmised that the group traveled to the Black Hills before arriving at Fort Berthold, while others assume the party had already been to the Black Hills and back before arriving at Fort Union. The details about Gore's activities in the Black Hills and Fort Union are based on actual accounts, but in many attempts to track the party after their time in those locations, numerous

Fort Union on the Missouri River, as depicted by artist Karl Bodmer, circa 1833. *Library of Congress, Prints and Photographs Division.*

assumptions have been made based on those accounts. One oft-repeated story says the party was robbed by the Sioux and forced to walk all the way to Fort Berthold naked. That was one of Roberts's many surmises; it was based on what might have been consistent with Sioux behavior at the time, but no one from Gore or his party ever described such events. Eyewitness accounts became scarce at that point of the expedition, as Bostwick evidently wasn't with Gore then and Bridger and Vasquez had already departed the party. Gore paid Bridger $1,350 for his services and Vasquez $400, according to Robert Campbell's papers.[190]

Many years later, Gore's obituary said he was "attacked by Indians, and almost single-handedly he kept them at bay until he was able under cover of night to make his escape," but that could be a glorified tribute. Upon Gore's return to St. Louis, one paper quoted him as saying the strife between tribes and settlers had never been worse, but no mention was made in the article of Gore being robbed.[191] The stories of the Gore party being plundered by Natives likely stemmed from Proteau's Black Hills account and a detail later recalled by Louis Sears, a former boat puller for the American Fur Company. Its competitor Frost, Todd and Company had hired Sears to work at the Gros Ventre Fur Trading Post, located across the Missouri River from Fort Berthold and run by a fur trader named John McBride.[192] Sears recalled that "an English nobleman, Sir George Gore, wintered in the vicinity of the trading post" and that "the Sioux had stolen all his horses and plundered his wagons leaving him without supplies."[193]

Gore had obviously escaped the alleged robbery with his life, but that detail was lost in the rumor mill at the time. In another letter from Vaughn to Cumming, issued in November 1856, Vaughn wrote that there were reports being circulated by "both Inds and whites that Sir George Gore and his party of twelve men has been murdered by the Blackfeet and Uncpapa Bands of Sioux while sojourning through their country."

Vaughn said he hoped the rumor wasn't true, but he also said he wouldn't be surprised if it was.

"That number of men and animals passing through the heart of their country killing and scattering the small quantity of game which is their only means of subsistence and the constant starved condition they are in, is absolutely enough to drive them to acts of desperation," Vaughn wrote.[194]

But the rumors of Gore's demise were exaggerated, and he arrived in the area of Fort Berthold and McBride's Gros Ventre Fur Trading Post apparently unharmed. Sears is recorded as saying that McBride then furnished Gore with the necessary outfit and supplies to help him survive through the winter.

Sears's account was published in the collections of the State Historical Society of North Dakota in 1906. In Bradley's 1870s-era retelling of Bostwick's account of the hunt, Bostwick said the Gore party had split into two groups after departing Fort Union and began heading to Fort Berthold, and while the land party was on its way to Fort Berthold, it "had some difficulty with the Hunkpapa, or Blackfeet Sioux, on the Little Missouri."[195]

It's possible that the land party was robbed, but Gore wasn't with them at the time, as he was later remembered to have floated down the Missouri River to Fort Berthold with Robert S. Gardner, a former Indian agent at Fort Berthold.

"Some thirty-three years ago," *The Washburn Leader* wrote of Gardner, in 1890, "while out on a pleasure hunt with Sir Saint George Gore, of Ireland, they rowed down the Missouri river, and lived principally on meat from August 1st to January 16th, having no bread to eat during that time, and subsequently, during that winter, paid $200 for a barrel of flour."[196]

The details of that memory align with Bostwick's recollection of Gore being charged high prices for food when he reached the American Fur Company traders at Fort Berthold, who were feuding with the Frost, Todd and Company traders at the Gros Ventre Fur Trading Post across the river.

Heldt, who was apparently not fond of the traders in the region, penned a comical recount of this situation in his 1876 story about Gore's expedition:

> *The trade of* [Fort Berthold] *was not immense, nor was it exceedingly lucrative, and the arrival of Sir George Gore was an event of no small moment, especially as his wants and those of his party were not inconsiderable, and his liberality bordered on extravagance. He had been purchasing his beeves of one of the prominent actors in the heady feud which had annihilated brotherly love in Berthold, at fifty dollars per head. If he was not unconscious of the fight going on, he certainly sought to disguise his nativity by remaining neutral. One day his beef contractor raised fifty per cent on his goods, whereupon the testy Sir George went to a rival dealer in herds, who charged him thirty dollars per head; whereupon, although he had no use for more than a half-dozen head, he purchased fifty head—perhaps with the view of inculcating a moral lesson. He became thenceforth a great favorite at Berthold, but we bear willing witness that this little essay of his in moral philosophy was seed sown in barren ground, and has not yet brought forth any fruit whatever.*[197]

The high food prices to which Gore was subjected were suggested by Bradley as the rationale behind Gore's decision to abandon the traders at Fort Berthold and the Gros Ventre Fur Trading Post. Gore spent the remainder of the winter living in an earth lodge with the Gros Ventres of the Missouri, otherwise known as the Hidatsa tribe. Chief Crow's Breast of the Hidatsa gave up his own residence to Gore, possibly because Gore was a "generous and eccentric stranger," as described by Heldt.[198]

The comical contradiction of Gore living in a mud and clay dwelling while a mansion awaited him back in Brighton was such a fascinating fish-out-of-water scenario that Johnson chose to name his book after it. *Baronet in an Earth Lodge* used previously undiscovered letters from fur trader Henry A. Boller to describe the settings Gore likely encountered on the Hidatsa's lands, as Boller was there the following winter.

"Almost at my feet, the frozen river, fringed on the opposite bank with a line of timber beyond which again rises, a row of lofty bluffs, terminating in a boundless prairie," Boller wrote, as transcribed by Johnson.[199]

The frozen river was the reason for Gore being forced to remain on the icy banks of the Upper Missouri River for the winter of 1856–57, as no steam ships would make the voyage upriver from St. Louis to Fort Berthold until it thawed. When it did, Gore boarded the steamer *St. Mary*,

An exterior view of an earth lodge in Glenwood, Iowa. *Bill Whittaker, Wikimedia Commons.*

An interior view of an earth lodge at Fort Abraham Lincoln State Park in North Dakota. *Gooseterrain2, Wikimedia Commons.*

Chief Crow's Breast (*left*) and Chief Poor Wolf of the Hidatsa tribe. *Wikimedia Commons.*

traveling down the Missouri River from Fort Berthold and reaching St. Louis in early June.

The *St. Mary* "brought down about twenty passengers, among them Sir George Gore, a British nobleman, who has been some years engaged in buffalo and bear hunting in the Crow country," *The St. Louis Globe Democrat* reported in June 1857. "Sir George is accompanied by a suite consisting of some eight persons, and brings down with him a large collection of bear, deer and buffalo skins and other valuable furs, besides a beautiful Indian dog."[200]

The article was favorable in its description of Gore.

"His experience of the wild life of the mountains and the plains has imparted to him somewhat of the sunburnt hue of the trapper, and his unpretentious and most affable demeanor partakes largely of what on this side of the Atlantic we understand as social democracy."[201]

7
THE CRUSTY OLD BACHELOR

While Gore is now infamous for his hunting expedition in the Rocky Mountains, the expedition itself didn't receive much news coverage at the time. Gore was a frequent flyer in the St. Louis newspapers in late 1853 and early 1854, but after adventuring out into the wilderness, he mostly dropped off the press radar until the expedition was reaching its end.

When the writer Forbes Parkhill suggested that the story would make a good movie, with the "*Arabian Nights* atmosphere of Gore's luxurious adventuring," he wasn't even fully aware of how well the Gore journey fits the classic story structure of setup and conflict before it hits the climactic resolution of Gore using his camp luxuries as fuel for a massive bonfire. With the new plot element we now know regarding Gore's shrewd conduct as an absentee landlord in Ireland during the Great Famine, there's an even darker setup to explain the part of his personality that would rather burn his valuables than see them used by those whom he perceived to be squeezing more money out of him.

Parkhill, ever the raconteur, was looking for *The Wildest of the West*, according to his book's title, but it was actually Barry C. Johnson, the fact-checking biographer, who noticed what an outstanding conclusion Gore's story had in its *Baronet in an Earth Lodge* scene.

Johnson also discovered a new detail about how long Gore stayed in the United States after he left that earth lodge, learning that Gore was still in St. Louis in 1858. That refutes a claim from another popular book about Gore,

A man atop a pile of bison skulls waiting to be ground into fertilizer or charcoal in Detroit, Michigan, in 1892. The animals' tongues and hides created its first commercial markets, and secondary industries were formed years later from the bones left behind by the fur trade. *Wikimedia Commons.*

Speaking Ill of the Dead: Jerks in Montana History, in which the authors wrote, incorrectly, that Gore was back in the United Kingdom "in time for the 1857 Scottish stag hunt."[202]

Johnson, in his discovery of the letters of fur trader Henry A. Boller, learned that Gore was still in Missouri in 1858, as Boller was staying at the same hotel as Gore and wrote about Gore being there with him. But Johnson left off there, unable to determine when Gore returned to the United Kingdom. Exactly when Gore departed St. Louis and arrived back in England "are questions that remain open," Johnson wrote.[203]

But we can now see, thanks to the recent digitization of nineteenth-century newspapers, that Gore ended up staying in Missouri until April 1858 before heading back up to Canada, retracing the route that took him to the United States some five years earlier. In these final months in Missouri, Gore was reported to have hunted waterfowl in the eastern part of the state, and from this part of his adventures, we get one of the greatest previously unknown tales, which adds to Gore's Hollywood-esque legend: a report of him killing eight thousand birds.

It's important to keep in mind, however, how much exaggeration has surrounded Gore throughout history. The simple fact that he is still referred to as "Lord Gore" exemplifies that point. While he was in the United States, he was called Sir George Gore in hundreds of newspaper articles, yet after he left, he somehow started to develop the moniker "Lord Gore," despite the fact that he wasn't a lord, only a baronet. The first reference of a hunter named "Lord Gore" being in the United States was published in 1860, two years after he left, and it seems to only compound from there. Aiding its proliferation was the fact that, prior to the publication of *Baronet in an Earth Lodge* in 1997, the only other biography about Gore was Roberts's heavily surmised work, which used "Lord Gore" in its title. So, for a long time, the name stuck. Johnson wrote that when Roberts chose to deliberately refer to Gore as a lord, despite knowing Gore was merely a baronet (and even pointing it out), he did so in an effort to improve the title of his book. The "or" sound repeated in both "lord" and "Gore" has a nice ring to it, which no doubt helped the spread of the misnomer.

Some of the other tales that are suspected of being exaggerated or altogether false include Gore's naked march to Fort Berthold, the report of him killing six thousand bison, his hiring of eight hundred Native workers to cut Gore Pass, his party's discovery of gold in the Black Hills and the assumption that Lord Charles William Wentworth Fitzwilliam accompanied him on the expedition. Those stories are investigated in the earlier chapters of this book.

But one story we have yet to examine is that which came from the wildly unreliable narrator Buffalo Bill Cody, who claimed he saw Gore departing Fort Leavenworth when he was just a child. It appears Cody shared a kinship—if not a friendly rivalry—with Gore through their mutual bloodlust for bison.

The extermination of the estimated twenty-one million to eighty-eight million bison that occurred in nineteenth century America, culminating with fewer than five hundred left in existence by the end of the 1880s, is one of the world's most shocking ecological disasters, and individual hunters like Gore and Cody have been blamed for the catastrophe. But commercial enterprises that created new markets for buffalo robes were responsible for far more bison slaughter than any one man could claim. Pierre Chouteau Jr. & Co. was reported to have purchased fifty thousand robes each spring, and the total number of bison killed commercially was said to have been ten times larger than that figure.[204] The U.S. government also ordered the widespread slaughter of bison as a way to deny Native populations an important source of food, and epidemics like Texas tick fever and the loss of range management by the Natives (who were also exterminated and displaced) could be to blame as well.[205]

Gore was accused of killing between 2,000 and 6,000 bison in the 1850s, and Cody earned his nickname by killing 4,282 bison during an eighteen-month period from 1867 to 1868 while contracted to supply meat to the workers building the Kansas Pacific Railroad.[206] Perhaps that is why Cody was drawn to Gore, calling him "a sportsman among a thousand" and writing about him in an 1894 edition of *Cosmopolitan Magazine*. Roberts's scores of surmises seem trivial in comparison to Cody's, as Cody seemed to barely get anything right about Gore's expedition in his article. In it, he wrote that Gore was accompanied by 200 men, 7 of whom were slaughtered by Native tribesmen, and that incident spurred Gore to proposition the U.S. government to "whip the entire Sioux nation at his own expense." None of this is likely true.

"Naturally enough," Cody continued, "Sir George's proposal could not be accepted, and the next year saw him hunting down in Florida where he led a large party of sportsmen and a big pack of hounds."[207]

Gore did eventually make it to Florida—but not until the 1870s on an entirely different adventure. The "next year" that Cody referenced (which we will assume to be the winter of 1857–58) instead saw Gore heading to the New Madrid area of eastern Missouri on a trip that has been entirely undiscovered prior to my research.

Gore was reported by the *New Madrid Times* to have arrived in southeastern Missouri in November 1857 with his attendants and hunting equipment. He then proceeded to "Pa-paw on Little River, six miles distant," according to the *Times*'s report. "We suppose at that place he will encamp for the sport of the winter. The ducks, geese, &c., are becoming very abundant, and from the number of guns, men and munitions of fowling, we suppose he will slay game by thousands."[208]

Some two decades later, the arc of Gore's legend on the Mississippi River extended into the pages of *The Indianapolis Journal*.

"The scarcity of wild ducks is owing in great measure to the destruction of the wild rice fields," the *Journal* reported on January 24, 1879. "To show the wholesale description of game in our western fields and waters, it is stated that in the winter of 1856 or 1857 Sir George Gore killed 8,000 waterfowl in the marshes of New Madrid county."[209]

Passengers aboard the Kansas-Pacific Railroad, depicted shooting buffalo from the cars of the train. An 1867 *Harper's Weekly* article describes how the train was "slowed to a rate of speed about equal to that of the herd" so passengers could shoot the animals with guns furnished by the railroad. *Library of Congress, Prints and Photographs Division.*

That incredible number, which Gore would have called 4,000 "brace," may seem too high to be true. But to a group like Gore and his men, who had seen such feats as Mr. Winsloe's 2,500 brace killed during a single hunting event in the fall of 1845, it would have been an entirely plausible achievement.

Gore returned to St. Louis following his duck derby in New Madrid during the spring of 1858, and then he headed back to Quebec during the summer. He was said to have been planning another fishing expedition in the Great Lakes, similar to the one with which he began his American adventure in 1853.

To return to Canada, Gore, it appears, reversed the route that he took to St. Louis in 1853, traveling through the Midwest. Some two decades after he left the United States, a dispatch in *The True Republican* newspaper in Sycamore, Illinois, recalled a visit from Gore that is characteristic of his reputation.

"Some of our older citizens will remember that some eighteen or twenty summers ago, Sycamore was visited by an English hunter who with his followers, servants, horses, dogs and guns put up at the old City Hotel and spent some weeks in hunting prairie chickens and other game in the country round," the *True Republican* reported in 1879. "He was Sir St. Geo. Gore, a British baronet of Inverness, Scotland, connected with some of the highest families of Europe and of immense wealth. He was an enthusiastic hunter, a crusty old bachelor, and he sumptered about our streets with his pants in his boots and quarreled with his landlord about his charges as if he wasn't worth $1,000."[210]

The prairie chicken story in Illinois is much like the buffalo story in the United States. When Gore was there, some ten million prairie chickens resided in the state. But hunting in Gore's time and habitat destruction a century later led to a dramatic drop in the animal's population, and by 1994, the Illinois Department of Natural Resources said there were only forty prairie chickens left in Illinois.[211]

After doing his part to rid Illinois of as many prairie chickens as he could, the crusty old bachelor who wore his pants tucked into his boots departed the United States, not to return until the 1870s. We know he reached Quebec in July 1858 with intentions to visit the Saguenay and Gulf fishing grounds, and accounts published in *The Liverpool Mercury* newspaper and *The London Gazette* show that Gore and five servants arrived back in England in November 1858 via the *Nova Scotian* steamship, which had departed Quebec in October 1858.

8
SEEKING EDEN

The articles regarding Gore's return to England raise a curious question. When Gore arrived in North America in 1853, he was reported to have landed in Canada with four servants, yet the documentation of his return to England says he arrived back home with five servants. It's possible that the newspapers got the details wrong—but it's also possible that Gore picked up another man along the way.

It would not have been the first time a British adventurer brought an American mountain man back to the United Kingdom with him. Two decades earlier, Sir William Drummond Stewart, the person suspected of giving Gore the idea to visit the American West, brought the hunter Antoine Clement back to Scotland with him after embarking on a Rocky Mountain tour of his own in the 1830s. Recently, it has been revealed that Stewart and Clement were lovers in a same-sex relationship, adding a new level of explanation to Stewart's effort to bring Clement back to Scotland with him. This is detailed in William Benemann's excellent book *Men in Eden*, in which Benemann reveals not just Stewart's homosexuality but also the likelihood that many mountain men in the Rocky Mountain fur trade were gay.

Stewart's homosexuality was somewhat overt for the time, yet Benemann found examples of previous writers who "felt it necessary to wrap Stewart in a protective cloak of respectable heterosexuality," even though he spent most of his life avoiding women and consorting with men.[212]

Like Stewart, Gore also spent his life with other men. Amid all the newspaper reports of Gore attending parties in the United Kingdom,

Left: Antoine Clement. *Wikimedia Commons.*

Right: Robert Campbell. *Wikimedia Commons.*

staying at swanky hotels and boarding yachts, I never found any mention of him being in the company of a woman. Also like Stewart, Gore has been portrayed as being unquestionably heterosexual by previous writers, who have not raised the possibility that he might have been gay despite a couple of possible suggestions buried in the source material.

Benemann made the case for several high-profile figures from the Old West who appeared to have been more than just friends or business associates, and he learned that Stewart was not the first highborn European traveler to bring a young member of the Rocky Mountain fur trade back to the old country with him. In the 1820s, Duke Paul Wilhelm of Würtemberg brought Jean-Baptiste Charbonneau, the son of the legendary Sacagawea, back to Germany with him when Charbonneau was eighteen years old. The two lived together and traveled the countryside for years, but not much is known about their relationship. A historian priest who was attempting to put together a more detailed biography of Charbonneau dropped the project after he said he heard a "loathsome" story about him in what was, perhaps, another example of a writer choosing to not share his suspicions about the sexuality of his subject.[213]

While the reason is not known, a writer who was attempting to put together a more complete picture of Gore's life also dropped his project.

Nothing appears to have survived from his research, but it has been said that the Colorado historian Herbert O. Brayer visited some surviving members of Gore's family during the first half of the twentieth century and gained considerable information about the baronet before choosing not to publish any of his findings.[214]

The partnership between fur traders turned St. Louis businessmen William Sublette and Robert Campbell was another relationship explored by Benemann. Campbell, who was one of Gore's primary contacts upon arriving in Missouri, was a banker and a real estate investor. Benemann found a good description of Campbell's relationship with Sublette in a little-known biography of Sublette, in which the author wrote that Campbell had forged, with Sublette, "a community…[of] feelings, wishes, tastes and dangers of brotherly proportions," and the couple "spent as much time together as possible, nursed each other in sickness, and planned for the future in harmony and accord." A few years later, when Campbell was ill, his brother wrote to Sublette for him, telling Sublette that Campbell was constantly talking about him and wished him to be by his side in his convalescence, as "he will never believe he can have any nurse to be compared with you."[215]

In the community of suspected gay men involved in the Rocky Mountain fur trade, Campbell (the St. Louis businessman) and Stewart (the Scottish baronet) are two of the most prominent figures. Gore is said to have been convinced to visit the Rocky Mountains by Stewart, and he contacted Campbell upon arriving in St. Louis, so, objectively speaking, if Gore himself was not explicitly part of that community, he was at very least connected with it.

While they were living together, Campbell and Sublette were also in business together, which provided cover for the partners in an era when living out of the closet was out of the question.

"They co-owned one of the most important trading businesses and were popular hosts, welcoming guests to their Sulphur Springs estate," Benemann writes.[216]

When Stewart brought Clement back to Scotland after his 1830s sojourn in the Rocky Mountains, he needed a cover to explain their closeness. Stewart had just inherited his Murthly Castle (becoming what the Scottish call a "laird"), which was his reason for returning to Scotland. Stewart "would occupy the castle, run the estate from his study there, entertain in the ballroom and music room—but in the evenings he and Clement would retire to the nearby Dalpowie Lodge, a spacious and well-appointed retreat on the estate where they could enjoy a high degree of privacy," Benemann wrote. "In public they would maintain a fiction that would allow them to live in intimate contact without necessarily making a challenging statement: Antoine Clement would be explained as Sir William's valet....There was no need to clarify further Antoine Clement's position in the new laird's life: a gentleman obviously required a valet."[217]

Gore, too, had a close companion with whom he spent much of his life, the fly tyer Alexander Mackenzie. Not much is known about Mackenzie, but his description as Gore's personal fly tyer presents a convenient reason for them to have spent a lot of time together. Mackenzie was described in Gore's obituary as being one of just a few people to attend his funeral, having "accompanied him on so many shooting and fishing expeditions." In an 1857 *New York Times* article, Gore said he needed Mackenzie along on his adventures because he desired to be in the company of "the most accomplished fly-maker in Europe."[218]

On Gore and Mackenzie's expedition to the Rocky Mountains, the hunting-obsessed Gore was obviously there to collect as many trophies as he could, but the party also insisted on making another stop: "an immense Crow camp of which they had heard."[219]

The Gore party's decision to seek out the Crows, of all the tribes in the area, may have been the result of the party's desire to visit the men well known as "the handsomest body of Indians in North America" who had "a good many berdashes among them, homosexuals who dressed and lived as [women]." The Crows, Benemann writes, were "a tribe for whom the tradition of the berdache was documented well into the twentieth century." And the berdashe (more commonly spelled "berdache") would often "catch the attention of white men who traveled the American West in hopes of finding a safe space for their homoerotic attractions."[220] The mid-nineteenth-century West is described by Benemann as an Eden for gay men looking to find a degree of freedom, and gay-tolerant Crow camps specifically helped make it the Eden that he described. This fact was well known among mountain men at the time, so one hint about Gore's sexuality that may have been hidden in the source material is the description of his party seeking out the Crow camp, where "they remained several days conversing with, if not enjoying the company of, several vagabond whites, who had become identified with the Crows."[221]

The Gore expedition is often described as being unique, but it doesn't sound altogether different than Stewart's lavish return to the Rockies in the 1840s, after he had achieved the financial means to embark on a fancy foray out west. Stewart departed Westport with approximately ninety men divided into groups of six, with each company allotted a two-wheeled cart that was pulled by two mules. Many of Stewart's friends were part of the group, and Sublette was the cocaptain of the entourage, despite his failing health.

Like Gore, Stewart had in tow a vast selection of exotic provisions. But unlike Gore, Stewart also brought a writer, Matthew C. Field, to document the trip. Field detailed Stewart's collection of various fine wines and liquors, coffee, cigars and ingredients to make gumbo and English plumb pudding, along with tiger skin carpets, sable robes, two India rubber boats for fording streams and dozens of tents of different shapes and colors. There was also one more bit of luggage that may have been puzzling to some of the guests who weren't aware of Stewart's plans for a grand finale: a collection of "old chivalrous costumes with large plumbed hats with rolled-up brims, jerkins with slit sleeves, leather leggings, tall riding boots with velvet greatcoats" and "the hat of an Italian brigand captain with red cock's features."[222]

Field also wrote about the erotic ways in which the men amused each other, doing things like posing nude in imitation of Greek statues, but he sometimes found the banter to be too much for him. In his diary, Field complained of the men's incessant sexual innuendos, writing "if one says 'I want to show you something,' your wit of this description will say, 'O, show your ass!'"[223]

When Gore "had met Sir William Drummond Stewart in Perthshire after his second trip and heard his stories of the buffalo, the bears, and the mountain men,"[224] as British historian Peter Pagnamenta wrote in *Prairie Fever: British Aristocrats in the American West*, a level of tolerance, thanks to Stewart, had already been established in the minds of those mountain men regarding the eccentricities of wealthy British aristocrats. Nevertheless, Gore's lifestyle still rubbed some the wrong way, which is where we find another suggestive detail buried in the source material about him. After returning to Missouri following his Rocky Mountain expedition, Gore took up residence in the Planter's House Hotel in St. Louis. Also staying there at the time was Henry A. Boller, the fur trader whose letters were uncovered in *Baronet in an Earth Lodge.* In the letters, Boller complained about the exceptionally private lifestyle Gore presented while living there, twice mentioning Gore's time spent bathing with his servant.

"I sincerely hope he will soon return to 'Hingland,'" Boller wrote, poking fun at Gore's accent. "Why this 'Sportsman' had a barber to shave him… and another man to rub and wash him down every morning after rising!"[225]

9

SINGLE IN THE SOUTHEAST

During Gore's first visit to the United States, he was in his forties, and no mind was paid to the fact that he was a bachelor. But when he returned in the 1870s, he was in his sixties, and the press found his still-unmarried status hard to ignore.

The account of Gore's 1850s visit written by George C. Heldt, published in 1876 in *The Historical Society of Montana Contributions*, is the only piece of source material on Gore that makes any mention of the British baronet's visit to the southeastern United States in the 1870s. That account says, simply, that Gore "in 1875 made a trip to the Everglades of Florida," but doesn't go into any more detail.[226]

The truth is Gore's return trip to the United States actually began much earlier, as we can now see from the newspapers of the time that have been digitized. And he visited many more places than the Everglades.

Gore arrived in Quebec in June 1873 with three servants via the *Sarmatian* steamship out of Liverpool.[227] He stayed throughout most of the fall season in Canada, where he was reported to be a guest of the St. Louis Hotel in Quebec and the Rossin House Hotel in Toronto. When he arrived in the United States, Gore began his next hunting expedition in the same place that his previous one had left off—New Madrid, Missouri, where he was rumored to have killed eight thousand birds. This time, however, Gore's sights were set on the Southeast, with New Madrid as his starting point. Gore informed *The British Whig* newspaper in Ontario that, upon leaving Canada in November 1873, he was headed for "a hunting expedition in Florida."[228]

The St. James Hotel in Jacksonville, Florida, circa 1890. *Detroit Publishing Co.; Library of Congress.*

For this expedition, Gore may have been motivated by the trend in crocodile hunting that was sweeping his British hunting circles. Numerous articles about alligator and crocodile hunting appeared alongside the ordinary hunting coverage in the sporting press in the 1860s, and in the February 1872 edition of the British magazine *Land and Water*, Lord Henry John Reynolds-Moreton, the third Earl of Ducie, shared a thrilling story of stalking a crocodile that had killed a young girl on the Nile River. Many years earlier, Lord Moreton was one of the "numerous and highly respectable assemblage of sporting noblemen and gentlemen" described alongside Gore in the *The Derby Mercury* as Gore was inheriting his baronetcy.

New Madrid is the only location Gore visited during both his 1850s and his 1870s hunting expeditions in the United States. It's a unique area known for the massive earthquakes that rocked the region in 1811 and 1812, the largest known earthquakes to have hit the United States east of the Rocky Mountains. Gore's fondness for New Madrid was most likely due to the fact that it was a good hunting area, where people would boast of big scores. Some of the nineteenth-century newspaper coverage to come out of New Madrid sounded a bit like the *Inverness Courier*'s coverage of the Glorious Twelfth.

"Deer, turkey, squirrels, rabbits, and ducks are very plentiful, but the ducks are hard to get at," the *St. Louis Globe-Democrat* reported from New Madrid on August 26, 1885. "A.C. Underhill says 'I take the medal for being the best frog-shooter in Southeast Missouri. I killed sixteen dozen frogs in seven hours and shipped them to you when you were selling them at $1.50 a dozen.'"

But Gore was interested in more than the area's renowned frog shooting opportunities when he arrived in New Madrid in 1873, and he began gearing up immediately. A December 11, 1873 dispatch from *The Cincinnati Commercial* newspaper reported that the dry dock firm Walker & Nellis built a skiff "which was forwarded last night to New Madrid, Missouri, for Sir George Gore and party to paddle around in the bayous, while on their hunting expedition." Gore had been seen in New Madrid a week earlier "with a carload of dogs," the *Commercial* added.[229]

After spending a month in the New Madrid area, Gore headed to New Orleans via the *Susie Silver* steamship, and the *Commercial* again reported on his doings, writing that he was "bound to the Everglades of Florida with 164 pkgs of trunks and other baggage, 21 dogs, 3 horses, and 6 biped attendants."[230]

At that time, the American press began speculating on Gore's income, which is not surprising considering how much luggage and crew he had with him. But what is surprising is how wildly the accounts differed.

In January 1874, when Gore arrived in Tennessee on the *Susie Silver,* the *Memphis Avalanche* reported that he was carrying "about 6,000 pounds of baggage," and "his income is a quarter of a million per year."[231] The *Commercial,* continuing to follow Gore's exploits, reported on January 20 that Gore's income "is said to be £7,000 per annum."

When detailing Gore's wealth, reporters couldn't seem to resist the inevitable subplot of his marital status. As he left Memphis on January 12 on the Memphis & Charleston Railroad, the *Avalanche* reported that Gore was "in search of pleasure, and will take it out in hunting, fishing, etc., in the glades of Florida," adding, "He can afford it; his income is a quarter of million per year, and he is not married."[232]

The Galveston Daily News, reporting that Gore was headed for Florida on January 17, wrote that Gore "is a bachelor, with a revenue of $35,000 a year."[233]

Several papers made jokes about Gore being single, the funniest example coming from the *Brooklyn Argus* newspaper, which wrote that Gore was "worth half a million per annum and still unmarried, waking the echoes of the Tennessee forests with his shot-gun while forty or fifty of the Memphis belles are said to be thirsting for him."[234] The *Boston Evening Transcript* said he was in town on a hunting excursion, but "the number of pretty Northern ladies at the hotels renders it advisable to 'hunt' chiefly in the drawing room."[235]

It may seem odd that those journalists used such sexually suggestive language when writing about an overweight sixty-two-year-old bachelor who was less than five years away from his own natural death, but Gore apparently didn't look so unhealthy. A reporter for *The Norfolk Virginian* newspaper, in an attempt to pen a physical description of Gore in 1874, greatly underestimated his age, calling him "a large and stately looking old gent, about fifty years old," adding that he "resembles a Kentucky farmer."[236] *The Public Ledger* called him "a fine looking specimen of an Englishman, weighing over two hundred pounds."[237]

Gore appears to have arrived in Jacksonville on schedule, staying there for some time in the company of his own ilk. The *Boston Evening Transcript*, in March 1874, reported that he was among several members of "the nobility of Great Britain" in Jacksonville, including Viscount Parker and the Earl of Dunraven (who later mentioned his time in Florida in his book *The Great Divide*).[238] It's unclear if Gore made it all the way to the Everglades on that trip, as he was reported to be on the *Lizzie Baker* steamship out of Palatka, Florida (about fifty miles south of Jacksonville), in April 1974, heading north.

"Sir St. George Gore, the English Lord whose passage through Savannah to Florida was some time since noted, returned on the *Lizzie Baker* Saturday, with his retinue and fixings," *The Atlanta Constitution* reported on April 28, 1874. "His freight bill amounted to $300, which was a reduction in consequence of its quantity. It is sad to mention that Sir St. George has to wrestle with the evils of this life on the paltry income of $400 per day."[239]

The following month, the story of Gore being mistaken for a drunken Irishman by the night watchman at the St. James Hotel in Jacksonville began being noted in papers across the country. As the story began circulating, Gore was reported to be a passenger on the *San Jacinto* steamship heading for New York in May 1874. He went to Canada from there, where he spent the summer and fall seasons of both 1874 and 1875.

In December 1874, Gore arrived back in the United States on a steamship from Quebec en route to Louisiana, "where he proposes to spend the winter in a hunting expedition," *The Norfolk Virginian* reported.

"He had with him two fine horses, four white servants, six dogs (three English retrievers, two pointers and an Irish setter) three guns, a large tent and everything else necessary to camping comfort."

The Sugar Bowl newspaper, in December 1874, reported that Gore had arrived in Louisiana "with a camping outfit and an array of supporters greater than Kellogg himself could command," in reference to the state's governor, William Pitt Kellogg.

"His camping outfit consists of nine large tents, with bedsteads, mattresses, center tables, stoves, carpets, etc., and every appurtenance necessary to comfort, and even luxury," *The Sugar Bowl* reported. "He is accompanied by six men, who load his guns, retrieve his game, and fish him out of alligator holes with in the field, and who chunk up the camp fires, broil his jack snipe, light his pip, dig the chiggers out of his legs, and scratch his back when he returns to the comfort of his princely camp."

The paper reported that Gore camped near Grosse Isle in Vermilion Parish, Louisiana, until the spring of 1875, "and it will require some ten or twelve wagons to transport his effects thither."

And again, at that time, there was yet another estimate of Gore's income that differed wildly from the others.

"Sir St. etc. has a daily income on eighteen hundred pounds sterling ($9,000), or $3,285,000 and no cents per annum, throwing out the odd hours, minutes, seconds, and so-forth," *The Louisiana Sugar Bowl* reported. "And the noble gentleman finds it much cheaper to kill his own game, and more agreeable to have it prepared under his own nose, than to live in hotel."[240]

Gore then left by train for Canada in the spring of 1875. He spent the summer and fall there and returned to the United States in time for the winter waterfowl season. *The Raleigh Sentinel* reported his arrival in December 1875, writing that he was duck hunting in Currituck County, North Carolina.[241] Gore's decision to hunt that area shows, once again, the talent he had for gathering beta on good hunting grounds. Kitty Hawk Bay (in that same area of North Carolina) would later be recognized as one of the finest duck hunting regions of the United States, despite being relatively unknown to hunters at the time. When "a party of New York gentlemen" founded, in 1881, the Kitty Hawk Bay Sportsmen's Club, newspapers across the country noted that the area had been "comparatively unvisited by sportsmen." But there were a couple of exceptions mentioned by name—the Grand Duke Alexis and Sir George Gore.[242]

After a few months of shooting what had to be hundreds (of brace) of ducks in the Kitty Hawk area, Gore finally journeyed back to England. In the stories of his departure, it was again mentioned that Gore was healthy-looking and unmarried.

"Among the departures from New York for Europe on Saturday was Sir George Gore, an old English baronet and a bachelor," *The Baltimore Sun* reported on February 26, 1876. "He is possessed of considerable wealth, and although now about sixty years of age, looks in his full vigor."[243]

Despite reports like that one, though, Gore did not have much time left. He died less than three years later on December 31, 1878, at the age of sixty-seven. His causes of death included congestion of the lung, a weak heart and an enlarged liver. He was in Scotland when he died, in the Inverness area, where he spent so many hunting seasons as a young man.

The only person with him at the time of his death was a gunmaker named Hugh Snowie, an old friend of Gore's who also wrote his obituary. The obituary said Gore was "famous as a sportsman in various parts of the world" and that it was "believed that he killed more big game in America than any man of his time."

10
NO SIR, NO SAINT

I was just a boy visiting his grandmother when I first became aware that the Gore Range in Colorado was one of the country's most beautiful mountain landscapes. She lived in Vail in view of the Gore, and I was watching the alpenglow illuminate its peaks when she told me she always thought it was one of the most spectacular ranges in America. She was a working-class local, a hostess at a restaurant in town, but she had managed to journey across the United States to many different ski areas before selecting a mountain town to settle on. This was back in the early 1970s, when such places were easier to pick up and move to.

I'm not sure what prompted me to ask her how the range got its name—probably the macabre situations in which the word *gore* is ordinarily applied—but it was at that moment that I first learned of Sir St. George Gore. In keeping with the tradition that persists to this day, her limited knowledge of him was totally inaccurate, and she told me he was Vail's first visitor. Later, she took me out to the Lord Gore Club, a restaurant in town, and we viewed the paintings of Gore that adorned its walls. The paintings were by the surmising author Jack Roberts, who was motivated to write his book about Gore after being commissioned by the restaurant to create portraits of its namesake. My grandmother seemed to be quite fond of Gore, his luxurious style and the fact that the area had so many landmarks named after him. I doubt it ever occurred to her that the potential for major problems existed in the way the town prioritized the business of wealthy tourists like Gore over the needs of local laborers like her.

Before-and-after images of the Sir St. George Gore monument atop Gore Pass in Colorado. *Photos by Randy Bishop and John LaConte.*

But that's the way it was in Vail at that time—and for many more years to come. And then something changed. Locals were pushed away from the economic center of the region, the so-called good jobs that were held by longtime residents were replaced by the low-paying positions of transient workers, corporations started acquiring the locally owned businesses and a backlash began to build against the community's long-held custom of catering to high-end clientele.

With that opposition came a re-evaluation of Gore's legacy in the minds of locals. When the Lord Gore Club restaurant opened in the 1960s, the silver-spoon status of its namesake was celebrated. Advertisements and articles about the restaurant touted its attempts to carry on Gore's reputation in its elegance. All the way into the 1990s, you could find a regular advertisement running in *The Vail Trail* newspaper that said Gore was accustomed to being served fine foods and choice wines nightly, and at the Lord Gore restaurant, the "legend lives on." But by the mid-2010s, the restaurant had changed its name and taken down all of Roberts's paintings. They're still on the property somewhere, a worker recently told me, locked away in a closet and no longer celebrated.

The restaurant's rebrand was a reflection of the changing attitudes about Gore that have taken hold in recent decades. In 2024, former Summit

County Commissioner Karn Stiegelmeier wrote a newspaper column about a proposal to change the name of the Gore Range to the Nuchu Range, "to honor the Ute people (Nuchu) who lived in this area for thousands of years before being forcibly removed to reservations following the Ute Removal Act that denied the Ute the 12 million acres of land that had formally been guaranteed to them in perpetuity."

Stiegelmeier said Gore's actions while hunting in the Rocky Mountains were "the opposite of our stewardship values today, and all those who helped guide him on his hunting journey were disgusted by his wastefulness, including Native Americans, mountain men, and the U.S. Calvary at the end of his trip."[244]

There is some source material on Gore that suggests otherwise—Chief Crow's Breast of the Hidatsa tribe gave up his own residence to Gore near the end of his journey; mountain man Jim Bridger "always commended [Gore] as a bold, dashing and successful sportsman"[245] and army Captain Randolph B. Marcy, who met Gore at the end of his trip in 1857, described him as "affable"[246]—but nevertheless, the negative feelings toward Gore expressed in Stiegelmeier's statement reflect many people's feelings in the community.

Gore's bad reputation is most apparent atop Gore Pass, where a bronze plaque in his honor, which has stood for seventy years, has been the subject

The sign from the former Lord Gore restaurant in Vail, Colorado, as seen on display at The Saloon in nearby Minturn. *Scott Cramer.*

of a rather intense act of vandalism. Using a welding torch and a file, the vandal was able to remove some of the cast bronze words from the plaque, which could not have been easy to do. I visited the site during June 2023 and discovered that it had been tampered with, but as I wasn't sure what the monument said originally, I had to scour the internet for a pre-vandalization picture of the plaque for comparison.

It was obvious that an adjective was removed from the front of the "George" in Gore's name, and part of me thought it might have been the word "Lord," as that prefix had been widely adopted and was incorrect. I finally found a picture taken by Colorado resident Randy Bishop in 2016 for his website www.peakbagger.com, which showed the plaque unmolested. I learned that the affected text was not the word "Lord," as I had suspected, it was Gore's proper title, "Sir St." I found the removal of that prefix to be a puzzling bit of activism, as Sir St. was never a controversial part of Gore's name. "St. George" was a common name during Gore's day (Lieutenant Colonel Philip St. George Cooke participated in the Harney Massacre in 1855), and the "Sir" title was indeed applied to baronets like Gore, so unlike "Lord Gore," "Sir St. George Gore" actually was his proper name. Removing the "Sir St." prefix didn't seem to make much sense, but nevertheless, someone went to great lengths to do it.

My theory is that because it has become so widely known that Gore was not a lord, yet everyone still calls him "Lord Gore," the vandals got stuck on the idea that Gore has had an incorrect prefix applied to his name and, knowing this, assumed the prefix on the plaque was wrong and sought to set the record straight.

Either that or the vandals chose to remove "Sir St." simply because they felt Gore was no sir and no saint.

Regardless, given the relatively small amount of information previously available about Gore, it would seem that Gore's only known transgression that would make someone upset enough to deface his plaque would have to be that he was "bent on slaughter of game," which is a turn of phrase that's actually written on the plaque directly underneath the now-removed Sir St. prefix. Never mind the fact that it was basically U.S. military policy at the time to rid the plains of bison in an effort to starve out Native tribes, Gore's excessive hunting is seen by many to be a bridge too far, and people have now gone to great lengths to remove his name from local landmarks and his titles from his monument.

I contacted the Grand County Sheriff's Office to see if they had received any reports of vandalization on Gore Pass. They said they had not. They asked me if I had reached out to the Routt County Sheriff's Office, as the county line between Routt and Grand Counties splits right where the plaque is located on Gore Pass. Routt County Sheriff administrative manager Kim Gittleson sent me the following response: "John, without a more specific location such as a mile marker on what road it would be an extremely large search to try and find out if we were contacted on this. I spoke with several deputies and they do not even know where this sign is located. You might want to start with the Forest Service or State Parks as they would be the owner of this sign."

I replied thirteen minutes later with an exact description of the road and mile markers, but Gittleson never responded. Contrary to Gittleson's assumption, the sign is not owned by the Forest Service or Colorado Parks and Wildlife. It's owned by History Colorado, formerly known as the State Historical Society of Colorado, which owns and maintains hundreds of similar monuments around the state.

History Colorado was not aware of the vandalism either. Luke Perkins, the organization's public relations professional, told me his office only learned about the incident thanks to my inquiry. Perkins said they know the plaque was fully intact as of 2019, because his office performed a field inspection at that time and had a record of inspection and photo from May 10, 2019. I asked him to send me the report, and you can imagine my surprise when I found the attached picture to be a duplicate of Randy Bishop's image from www.peakbagger.com! It was lifted off his site in the exact file size you get from right clicking and selecting "save image as."

In contacting Bishop and Perkins about the picture, we all agreed that the inspection photo was indeed a copy of Bishop's photo from 2016. I pressed Perkins to tell me if his inspector had admitted to using Bishop's photo or not, and while I didn't get an answer, Perkins did acknowledge that I had the right to be suspicious of the inspection's accuracy. He put me in touch with Patrick Eidman, the deputy state historic preservation officer, who said inspectors try to get an original photo of their plaques at the time of inspection, but that's not always possible.

"There are certainly times when we will pull photos that others have taken, if it's a good shot that shows the text," Eidman said. "Those bronze plaques, in particular, are hard to photograph, it just depends on the lighting and time of day."

Eidman said, as a best practice, inspectors should indicate in their reports if they did not take the photo themselves, but he was not sure if that occurred in this case.

Bishop said he also visited the plaque in 2017, saw it unmolested at that time and had a photo from that trip. So, the photo evidence shows the vandalization occurred sometime between Bishop's 2017 visit and my 2023 visit, but exactly when it happened, or who did it "are questions that remain open," in the words of Gore's previous biographer.

What we do know is that a portable welding torch and file were brought all the way up to a remote location miles from any town or settlement and used to shear the prefix off Gore's name some 163 to 170 years after he visited that location. It's a testament to the lasting power of his legacy that Gore has managed to inspire this type of controversy into the twenty-first century—and all because people are upset that he killed too many animals. Imagine if they knew that he was an absentee landlord during the Great Famine, evicting starving tenants from his confiscated lands.

EPILOGUE

It's been said that nothing exceeds like excess. And in Colorado, the embodiment of that statement is Gore, a man defined by his excesses who has exceeded as a namesake for generations.

How did that happen, you ask?

Blame it on America's most beloved mountain man, Jim Bridger.

Bridger was so well respected, so reliable as a guide—and so impressive was the map of the West that existed in his head (far superior to the physical maps of his day)—that when he coined the name for Gore Pass, the name stuck.

By turning a footpath into the region's first mountain pass road before his very eyes, Gore accomplished an amazing feat, but it was his reason for doing so which must have shocked Bridger the most. Gore built Gore Pass purely for the pleasure of his recreational pursuits, hiring a labor force and creating not just a road but a roving hub of economic activity which surrounded him as he undertook his adventures.

And in that way, the naming of that pass was symbolic of the relentless march of capitalism that was coming for the area in the form of outdoor tourism. Wreckreation on vacation, Gore created temporary markets in the places where his excessive hunting expedition exceeded, and Bridger was one of the locals who benefited from those new markets. The road was the evidence of the perceived progress that this influx of outdoor recreation tourism left in its wake, henceforth Bridger named that road after the man who opened his eyes to the possibility of a new economic driver for the region.

In the future, those same principles would be put into play across the state, and nowhere better embodies this than Vail, Colorado, which sits beside Gore Creek in the shadow of the Gore Range.

The ski town of Vail and the massive international conglomerate of Vail Resorts (NYSE: MTN) was also created entirely from an outdoor recreation market, attracting wealthy foreign tourists just like Gore. And it was also named after the builder of the road that took the tourists there, state highway engineer Charles Vail, who built Vail Pass.

Bridger, in his many travels and guiding gigs, was known for his uncanny ability to predict the future. He knew when bad weather was on its way, when one route would favor another, and—most tragically (for his foresight was not heeded)—when war was on the horizon between settlers and Native tribes.

But in naming the region's first mountain pass road after Gore, who was western Colorado's first wealthy tourist seeking outdoor recreation, Bridger might have made his most lasting prediction. Outdoor recreation tourism and all its excesses are here to stay.

NOTES

Chapter 1

1. "A Blue-Blooded Rooster," *The Sun*, May 9, 1874.
2. "The Great American Desert," *The Colorado Transcript*, January 9, 1867.
3. Edward Berthoud, "Results Obtained by the Survey of the New Route for the Overland Travel and Mail, from the Valley of the South Platte to Provo and Great Salt Lake," *The Daily Rocky Mountain News*, October 12, 1861.
4. "The Powell Expedition," *The Daily Rocky Mountain News*, September 1, 1868.
5. Barry C. Johnson, *Baronet in an Earth Lodge* (The English Westerners' Society, 1997), 1.

Chapter 2

6. "Passengers in the Steamer *Lady Eglinton*, from Liverpool," *Ottawa Daily Citizen*, July 9, 1853.
7. "*Lady Eglinton*," Scottish Built Ships, https://www.clydeships.co.uk/view.php?ref=18450.
8. "Steam Direct to Canada," *Liverpool Mercury*, July 19, 1853.
9. "Hunting Party," *Poughkeepsie Journal*, December 10, 1853.
10. "Heavy Robbery," *The Louisville Daily Courier*, December 7, 1853, citing *The St. Louis News.*
11. "Assorted Dogs," *The Lafayette Daily Courier*, December 12, 1853, citing *The Missouri Republican.*
12. "A Nobleman's Traps," *Galena Daily Advertiser*, February 22, 1854, citing *The St. Louis Intelligencer.*
13. "News from Colonel Fremont's Party," *New York Daily Herald*, March 20, 1854, citing *The St. Louis Republican.*

14. "Return the Hon. Charles Fitzwilliam," *Sheffield and Rotherham Independent*, May 6, 1854.
15. *Denver Evening Post*, August 20, 1897.

Chapter 3

16. Forbes Parkhill, *The Wildest of the West* (Henry Holt and Company, 1951), 131.
17. *Daily Ohio State Journal*, June 20, 1854.
18. "Nursed and Taught by Kansas Indians," *The Kansas City Star*, December 15, 1912.
19. "The Big Hunt of Sir George Gore," *The Cattleman Magazine* 39, no. 3 (August 1952): 118.
20. "A Celtic Nimrod in the Old West," *Montana, the Magazine of Western History* 9, no. 2 (Spring 1959): 56–66.
21. "Nursed and Taught," *Kansas City Star.*
22. Sam Wellman, *Thomas Johnson of Shawnee Mission* (Wild Centuries Press, 2020), chap. 9, Kindle.
23. Margaret Littman, "The Legacy and Future of Shawnee Indian Manual Labor Boarding School," National Trust for Historic Preservation, November 13, 2023, https://savingplaces.org/stories/the-legacy-and-future-of-shawnee-indian-manual-labor-boarding-school.
24. "U.S. Indian Boarding School History," National Native American Boarding School Healing Coalition, https://boardingschoolhealing.org/education/us-indian-boarding-school-history.
25. Littman, "Legacy and Future."
26. Wellman, *Thomas Johnson*, preface.
27. Jack Roberts, *The Amazing Adventures of Lord Gore: A True Saga from the Old West* (Sundance Publications, 1977), 24–26.
28. "Boston Adams, a Gentleman of the Old School," *The Kansas City Star*, October 21, 1906.
29. "Boston Adams," *The Kansas City Star.*
30. "Death of John F. A. Sanford," *Chicago Tribune*, May 11, 1857.
31. "Murder of Rev. Thomas Johnson," *Kansas City Weekly Journal*, January 7, 1865.

Chapter 4

32. "The Works of Hubert Howe Bancroft," in *History of Nevada, Colorado and Wyoming, 1540–1888* (The History Company, 1890), 696.
33. Berthoud, "Results Obtained."
34. Roberts, *Amazing Adventures*, 102.
35. *The Daily Rocky Mountain News*, August 19, 1863.

36. "Work to Begin on the Historic Gore Pass Road," *The Steamboat Pilot*, May 19, 1920.
37. "Gen. Hughes Dream to Be Realized," *The Steamboat Pilot*, October 8, 1902.
38. "The Powell Expedition," *The Chicago Tribune*, October 26, 1868.
39. "The Powell Expedition," *The Daily Rocky Mountain News*, May 14, 1869.
40. "The Powell Expedition," *The Daily Rocky Mountain News*, September 1, 1868.
41. "Western Colorado," *The Colorado Miner*, December 8, 1870.
42. Katrina Martin, "11 Million Tons Coal/Year Produced by Routt's Mines," *Steamboat Pilot*, July 22, 1998.
43. Robert Tann, "Controversial Oil Rail Project Back On Track," *Vail Daily*, May 30, 2025.
44. "Outline of the Railway Over the Range," *The Daily Rocky Mountain News*, February 11, 1877.
45. "Gore of the Gore Range," *Georgetown Courier*, August 28, 1897.
46. "For Automobile to Northwest Colorado," *The Steamboat Pilot*, July 31, 1912.
47. "Work to Begin," *The Steamboat Pilot*.
48. "Gore Pass Highway to Be Opened Soon for Motor Travel," *The Daily Rocky Mountain News*, May 24, 1920.
49. F. George Heldt, *Contributions of the Historical Society of Montana* (Historical Society of Montana, 1876), 148.

Chapter 5

50. Story from *Hunter-Trader-Trapper* magazine, reprinted by scores of newspapers across the United States, 1924.
51. Johnson, *Baronet*, 5.
52. "The Gores," *Cambridge Weekly News*, January 18, 1879, citing *The Echo*.
53. Robert Divine, T.H. Breen, George M. Fredrickson and R. Hal Williams, *America: Past and Present*, vol. 1, *To 1877*, 6th ed. (New York: Longman, 2002), 26–27.
54. Donald Akenson, *The Irish Education Experiment* (Routledge, 1970), 33–34.
55. Akenson, *Irish Education Experiment*, 35.
56. Akenson, *Irish Education Experiment*, 155.
57. "State of the South," *Glasgow Herald*, October 22, 1849, citing *King's County Chronicle*.
58. Colonel W.F. Butler, *The Great Lone Land: A Narrative of Travel and Adventure in the North-West of America* (Sampson Low, Marston, Low & Searle, 1872), 241.
59. John R. Cook, *The Border and the Buffalo* (Crane & Company, 1907), 113.
60. Ralph Leonard, "History on Horseback: Napoleon Bonaparte," *Quillette*, December 4, 2023, https://quillette.com/2023/12/04/history-on-horseback-napoleon-bonaparte.
61. "Large Gun," *Glasgow Herald*, March 25, 1844.
62. "Death of Sir St. George Gore," *Inverness Courier*, January 2, 1879.

63. Johnson, *Baronet*, 11–13.
64. "The Falls of Doonass," *Clonlara Community Heritage*, https://clonlara.clareheritage.org/places/the-falls-of-doonass.
65. "Limerick, April 5," *Coventry Standard*, April 14, 1837, citing *Limerick Chronicle.*
66. "The Moors," *The Morning Chronicle*, August 22, 1840, citing *Inverness Courier.*
67. "The Moors," *The Morning Chronicle*, August 22, 1840.
68. "Grouse Shooting—Inverness," *Caledonian Mercury*, August 19, 1841, citing *Inverness Courier.*
69. "Amongst the Sporting Feats," *The Era*, October 3, 1841.
70. "Death of Sir Ralph Gore, Bart.," *The Morning Post*, March 31, 1842.
71. "Extraordinary Sale of Sporting Dogs," *The Derby Mercury*, May 18, 1842.
72. "The Moors," *Caledonian Mercury*, July 23, 1842.
73. "Angling," *Aberdeen Journal*, August 24, 1842.
74. "Sporting," *Caledonian Mercury*, October 22, 1842.
75. "The Moors," *Aberdeen Journal*, August 23, 1843.
76. "Large Deer," *Caledonian Mercury*, September 28, 1843.
77. "Inverness," *Glasgow Herald*, August 23, 1844, citing an August 21 story from *Inverness Courier.*
78. "Field Sports of the North," *Glasgow Herald*, September 13, 1844, citing *Inverness Courier.*
79. "Grouse Shooting and Deer Stalking," *Caledonian Mercury*, October 3, 1844, citing *Inverness Courier.*
80. "Salmon Fishing," *Caledonian Mercury*, July 17, 1845, citing *Inverness Courier.*
81. "The Moors," *Glasgow Herald*, September 5, 1845, citing *Inverness Courier.*
82. "The Moors," *Caledonian Mercury*, September 18, 1845, citing *Inverness Courier.*
83. Peter Pagnamenta, *Prairie Fever: British Aristocrats in the American West, 1830–1890* (W.W. Norton & Company, 2012), 101
84. "The Moors," *The Times*, September 26, 1843, citing *Inverness Courier.*
85. "The Moors," *The Morning Chronicle*, August 29, 1844, citing *Ross-shire Advertiser.*
86. "The Moors," *The Standard*, August 28, 1845, citing *Inverness Courier.*
87. "Sporting," *The Morning Chronicle*, October 8, 1845, citing *Ross-shire Advertiser.*
88. "The Moors," *The Morning Post*, December 9, 1845, citing *Edinburgh Post.*
89. "The Moors," *Caledonian Mercury*, December 22, 1845, citing *Inverness Courier.*
90. "The Shooting Season," *Caledonian Mercury*, August 6, 1846, citing *Inverness Courier.*
91. "The Moors and Deer Forests," *Glasgow Herald*, August 28, 1846, citing *Inverness Courier.*
92. "Deer Stalking and Grouse Shooting," *Caledonian Mercury*, September 7, 1846, citing *Inverness Courier.*
93. "Sporting in the Highlands," *Glasgow Herald*, September 18, 1846, citing *Inverness Courier.*
94. "Deer Stalking," *Caledonian Mercury*, October 8, 1846, citing *Inverness Courier.*

95. "Deer Stalking," *Glasgow Herald*, November 2, 1846, citing *Inverness Courier.*
96. "Red Deer," *Caledonian Mercury*, August 16, 1847, citing *Inverness Courier.*
97. "News From the Hills—The Twelfth of August," *Glasgow Daily Mail*, August 20, 1847.
98. "Unrivalled Deer Stalk," *The Leicestershire Mercury*, September 25, 1847.
99. "Deer Stalking," *Aberdeen Journal*, September 22, 1847.
100. Harding Cox, *The History of Coursing: The Waterloo Cup* (Read Country Books, 2013), 4–7.
101. "Sales by Auction," *The Morning Post*, June 14, 1848.
102. "Waterloo Coursing Meeting," *The Morning Post*, March 4, 1848.
103. Helen Litton, *The Irish Famine, an Illustrated History* (Wolfhound Press, 1994), 52.
104. Litton, *Irish Famine*, 9–10.
105. Litton, *Irish Famine*, 22.
106. Litton, *Irish Famine*, 94–98.
107. "European Intelligence," *The Daily Republic*, November 7, 1849.
108. "European Intelligence," *The Daily Republic.*
109. "Murder of Mr. Cage," *The Belfast News Letter*, October 19, 1849, citing *Evening Packet.*
110. "The King's County Chronicle," *The Morning Post*, October 20, 1849.
111. "Murder of Mr. Cage," *The Standard*, November 16, 1849.
112. "Ashdown Park Coursing Meeting," *Jackson's Oxford Journal*, December 8, 1849.
113. "Ashdown Park Coursing Meeting," *The Morning Post*, February 11, 1850.
114. "Sales by Auction," *The Morning Post*, March 26, 1851.
115. "Passengers in the Steamer *Lady Eglinton*," *Ottawa Citizen.*
116. "Mrs. Henry J. Low Is Dead at Montreal," *The Ottawa Citizen*, February 25, 1925.

Chapter 6

117. Johnson, *Baronet*, 1.
118. "Celtic Nimrod," *Montana, the Magazine of Western History*, 56–66.
119. Parkhill, *Wildest of the West*, 130.
120. James H. Bradley, "Sir George Gore's Expedition," in *Contributions to the Historical Society of Montana*, vol. 11 (Historical Society of Montana, 1923), 246–51. Bradley's source is Henry Bostwick, but his dates are off by a year, detailing all of Bostwick's memories as occurring a year sooner than they actually happened.
121. Bradley, "Gore's Expedition," 246–51.
122. "Westward Ho!" *The New York Times*, February 27, 1857.
123. *Daily Ohio State Journal*, June 20, 1854.
124. Eugene F. Ware's *The Indian War of 1864* was originally published in 1911, but the University of Nebraska Press published a reprint in 1994.

125. Heldt, *Contributions*, 144.
126. Bradley, "Gore's Expedition," 247.
127. Randolph B. Marcy's *Thirty Years of Army Life on the Border* was originally published in 1866, but J.B. Lippincott published a reprint in 1963.
128. Jerry Enzler, *Jim Bridger, Trailblazer of the American West* (University of Oklahoma Press, 2021), 198.
129. *Denver Evening Post*, August 20, 1897.
130. "Nobleman's Traps," *Galena Daily Advertiser.*
131. Johnson, *Baronet*, 40.
132. H.C. Beeler, *Mineral and Allied Resources of Albany County, Wyoming, and Vicinity* (The Laramie Republican Co. Printers), 79.
133. *Denver Evening Post*, August 20, 1897.
134. Parkhill, *Wildest of the West*, 133.
135. Johnson, *Baronet*, 41, 67.
136. "Talk of Old Times," *The Oregonian*, November 12, 1888, citing *North American Review.*
137. Enzler, *Jim Bridger*, 244–45.
138. Roberts, *Amazing Adventures*, 6.
139. Marcy, *Thirty Years*, 403.
140. "Noted Frontiersman James Bridger," *Chicago Tribune*, January 15, 1872.
141. Parkhill, *Wildest of the West*, 134.
142. Johnson, *Baronet*, 38.
143. "Sir George Gore Led Hunting Trip Through Northwest Colorado in 1855," *The Steamboat Pilot*, July 30, 1964.
144. "Col. Fremont and His Party," *Buffalo Courier Express*, March 23, 1854, citing *St. Louis Republican.*
145. "Hughes Dream," *The Steamboat Pilot.*
146. "Gore Led Hunting Trip," *The Steamboat Pilot.*
147. *The Daily Rocky Mountain News*, October 9, 1865.
148. *Daily Ohio State Journal*, June 20, 1854.
149. "Very Late from the Upper Missouri," *St. Louis Globe Democrat*, June 13, 1857.
150. Enzler, *Jim Bridger*, 199.
151. Heldt, *Contributions*, 145.
152. Bradley, "Gore's Expedition," 247.
153. Campbell Papers, Letterbook 1-06:294, Mercantile Library, St. Louis, provided by Jerry Enzler.
154. Campbell Papers, Letterbook 1-06:294.
155. *The Harney Expedition Against the Sioux: The Journal of Captain John B.S. Todd* (Nebraska State Historical Society, 1962), 89–130.
156. *Harney Expedition*, 89–130.
157. Emerson Gifford Taylor, *Gouverneur Kemble Warren: The Life and Letters of an American Soldier, 1830–1882* (Houghton Mifflin, 1932), 28.

158. Mari Sandoz, *Crazy Horse: The Strange Man of the Oglalas* (University of Nebraska Press, 1992), 80–84, 328.
159. "From Fort Laramie," *Columbia Herald-Statesman*, November 2, 1855, citing *St. Louis Republican*.
160. Heldt, *Contributions*, 145.
161. Marcy, *Thirty Years*, 403.
162. Bradley, "Gore's Expedition," 249.
163. Bradley, "Gore's Expedition," 249.
164. Marcy, *Thirty Years*, 403–4.
165. "Celtic Nimrod," *Montana, the Magazine of Western History*, 64–65.
166. "Our Expeditionary Correspondence," *The New York Herald*, November 15, 1857.
167. Marcy, *Thirty Years*, 403.
168. "Col. Gore and the Duke of Wellington," *Bristol Times and Bath Advocate*, January 31, 1852.
169. Bradley, "Gore's Expedition," 247.
170. Bradley, "Gore's Expedition," 247.
171. Bradley, "Gore's Expedition," 246–51.
172. "Reminiscences of Fox Terriers and Fox Terrier Men," *The Fanciers' Journal*, August 15, 1891.
173. Bradley, "Gore's Expedition," 247.
174. Bradley, "Gore's Expedition," 247.
175. Enzler, *Jim Bridger*, 286.
176. "Gold in the Black Hills," *Carson Daily Appeal*, June 5, 1875.
177. "The Black Hills," *The Chicago Tribune*, April 10, 1875.
178. Bradley, "Gore's Expedition," 251.
179. Parkhill, *Wildest of the West*, 129.
180. Johnson, *Baronet*, 49.
181. Johnson, *Baronet*, 50.
182. Bradley, "Gore's Expedition," 250.
183. Johnson, *Baronet*, 50.
184. Johnson, *Baronet*, 54.
185. Heldt, *Contributions*, 146.
186. Heldt, *Contributions*, 146.
187. Johnson, *Baronet*, 55.
188. Roberts, *Amazing Adventures*, 7.
189. Roberts, *Amazing Adventures*, 171.
190. Enzler, *Jim Bridger*, 202.
191. "Very Late," *St. Louis Globe Democrat*.
192. Joseph L. Gavett, *Guardians of the Frontier: The Cross Family Chronicle, 1836–1903* (Xlibris Publishing, 2011), 104–5.
193. Roberts, *Amazing Adventures*, 183.

194. Johnson, *Baronet*, 52.
195. Bradley, "Gore's Expedition," 249.
196. *The Washburn Leader*, November 29, 1890.
197. Heldt, *Contributions*, 147.
198. Heldt, *Contributions*, 147.
199. Johnson, *Baronet*, 60.
200. "Very Late," *St. Louis Globe Democrat*.
201. "Very Late," *St. Louis Globe Democrat*.

Chapter 7

202. *Speaking Ill of the Dead: Jerks in Montana History* (Twodot, 2000), 30.
203. Johnson, *Baronet*, 64.
204. Enzler, *Jim Bridger*, 202.
205. "Reinterpreting the 1882 Bison Population Collapse," *Rangelands Magazine* 40, no. 4 (August 2018): 106–14.
206. Pagnamenta, *Prairie Fever*, 3.
207. "Famous Hunting Parties of the Plains," *Cosmopolitan Magazine* 17, no. 2 (June 1894): 131–42.
208. "A Hunting Party," *The Times-Picayune*, November 8, 1857, citing *The New Madrid Times*.
209. *The Indianapolis Journal*, January 24, 1879.
210. *The True Republican*, January 29, 1879.
211. "Greater Prairie-Chicken," Illinois Department of Natural Resources, https://dnr.illinois.gov/education/wildaboutpages/wildaboutbirds/wildaboutbirdsquail/wabgreaterprairiechicken.htm.

Chapter 8

212. William Benemann, *Men in Eden: William Drummond Stewart and Same Sex Desire in the Rocky Mountain Fur Trade* (Bison Books, 2012), 4.
213. Benemann, *Men in Eden*, 133–34.
214. Johnson, *Baronet*, 21.
215. Benemann, *Men in Eden*, 63–64, 96.
216. Benemann, *Men in Eden*, 65.
217. Benemann, *Men in Eden*, 220.
218. "Westward Ho!" *The New York Times*.
219. Heldt, *Contributions*, 145.
220. Benemann, *Men in Eden*, 104–5.
221. Heldt, *Contributions*, 146.
222. Benemann, *Men in Eden*, 267.

223. Benemann, *Men in Eden*, 261.
224. Pagnamenta, *Prairie Fever*, 102.
225. Johnson, *Baronet*, 63.

Chapter 9

226. Heldt, *Contributions*, 144.
227. "Birds of Passage," *The Montreal Star*, June 25, 1873.
228. "Canadian," *The British Whig*, November 24, 1873.
229. "The Rivers," *Cincinnati Commercial*, December 11, 1873.
230. *Public Ledger*, January 12, 1874.
231. "A Rich Englishman Out Shooting," *The Chicago Tribune*, January 22, 1874, citing *The Memphis Avalanche*.
232. "Englishman Out Shooting," *The Chicago Tribune*.
233. *The Galveston Daily News*, January 17, 1874.
234. *Cincinnati Commercial*, December 11, 1873, citing *Brooklyn Argus*.
235. *Boston Evening Transcript*, March 4, 1874.
236. "A Distinguished Arrival," *Norfolk Virginian*, December 1, 1874.
237. *Public Ledger*, January 13, 1874.
238. *Boston Evening Transcript*, March 4, 1874.
239. *The Atlanta Constitution*, April 28, 1874.
240. "A Noble Sportsman and His Retinue," *The Atlanta Constitution*, December 30, 1874, citing *The Louisiana Sugar Bowl*.
241. *The Raleigh Sentinel*, December 28, 1875.
242. "A Sportsmen's Paradise," *San Francisco Chronicle*, July 23, 1881.
243. "A Mighty Hunter," *The Baltimore Sun*, February 26, 1876.

Chapter 10

244. Karn Stiegelmeier, "Looking into the History of Names in Eagle County," *Summit Daily News*, March 2, 2024.
245. Marcy, *Thirty Years*, 403.
246. Marcy, *Thirty Years*, 403.

ABOUT THE AUTHOR

John LaConte is a reporter for the *Vail Daily* newspaper and the winner of the Colorado Press Association's award for best investigative news package in 2023. He lives in Vail, Colorado, with his wife and two children. This is his first book.